Accident and Emergency Radiology
X-ray interpretation

Chris Harvey
BSc(Hons) MBBS MRCP FRCR
Consultant Radiologist,
Hammersmith Hospital, London UK

Declan O'Regan
BSc MBBS MRCP FRCR PhD
Senior Lecturer,
Hammersmith Hospital, London UK

Steve Allen
BSc(Hons) MBBS MRCS FRCR
Consultant Radiologist,
Royal Marsden Hospital, London UK

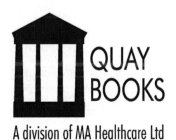

QUAY
BOOKS

A division of MA Healthcare Ltd

Quay Books Division, MA Healthcare Ltd, St Jude's Church, Dulwich
Road, London SE24 0PB

British Library Cataloguing-in-Publication Data
A catalogue record is available for this book

© MA Healthcare Limited 2009
ISBN 10: 1-85642-315-8
ISBN 13: 978-1-85642-315-1

Printed in the UK by CLE, Huntingdon, Cambridgeshire

ΠΑΤΕ ΠΙ

Accident and Emergency Radiology
X-ray interpretation

Contents

Preface

An accident and emergency attachment usually occurs early in a junior doctor's training. The combination of little formal training in the interpretation of radiographs, limited clinical experience, suboptimal anatomical knowledge, the stressful casualty environment and the litigious climate we practise under can make this a harrowing experience.

While the presence of a fracture is often evident clinically, a radiological assessment is essential to define the nature and extent of the injury as well as any associated soft tissue injuries. However, more importantly, radiography is necessary to diagnose unsuspected fractures and exclude bone injuries.

While radiological modalities have made huge technological advances in recent years, plain films remain the bread and butter in the initial assessment of the acutely injured patient. It is for these reasons that a sound grasp of emergency X-rays is essential. The interpretation of films requires a thorough and systematic approach. The purpose of this book is to show how a systematic analysis of accident and emergency radiographs allows the correct diagnosis to be derived while minimising errors.

This book is aimed at accident and emergency doctors, surgical, medical and radiology specialist registrars and medical students. This lavishly illustrated pocket sized book facilitates instant consultation when faced with an X-ray. At the start of each chapter there is a description of the relevant anatomy followed by a quick and easy yet detailed systematic approach to all types of X-rays likely to be encountered in the accident and emergency department. The book is illustrated with easy to follow line diagrams as well as fully annotated illustrative examples and is divided into concise chapters covering a particular region or problem. In addition to providing a systematic approach to the interpretation of the X-ray, tables provide instant access to lists and there are useful tips and hints in avoiding mistakes. There is also a list of key points at the end of each chapter. We hope this book will make the emergency film less daunting and so improve patient management

We thank our wives and children for their unwavering continued support

CHAPTER I

Interpretation of accident and emergency films: Basic principles

Description of fractures

Fractures of the long bones in adults are described using universally accepted conventions.

Fractures may be divided into **open** (the fracture is in communication with the external environment via a skin defect) and **closed** (the overlying skin is intact). These are usually diagnosed clinically but radiological signs such as gas in the soft tissues may be seen in open fractures.

A fracture may be **complete** (involving both cortices) or **incomplete** (when the fracture does not extend across the whole bone, e.g. greenstick fractures in children, see *Chapter 14*).

The site of the fracture should be described in terms of whether it is proximal, middle or distal along the bone shaft.

Types of fractures include **comminuted**, more than two separate fragments; **intra-articular**, involving the articular surface; and **impacted**, one fragment is driven into the other (*Figure 1.1*).

A fracture can be described as **transverse** (at 90 degrees to the long axis of the bone), **oblique** (at an angle of less than 90 degrees to the long axis) or **spiral** (curving along the bone shaft) (*Figure 1.1*).

Displacement of the distal fracture fragments is described relative to the proximal fragment. Displacement may be either anterior/posterior or medial/lateral (*Figure 1.2*).

Angulation describes the direction of tilt of the distal fracture fragment relative the proximal fragment (*Figure 1.2*).

Rotation of the fracture fragments may be described when the joints above and below the fracture are included on the film. The fracture may be internally or externally rotated.

An **avulsion** fracture refers to the separation of a bone fragment at the site of attachment of a ligament or tendon. Common sites of this type of injury are the ankle and fingers.

   Displacements of the joint are described as **dislocated** (complete separation of articular surfaces) or **subluxed** (partial contact of the articular surfaces).

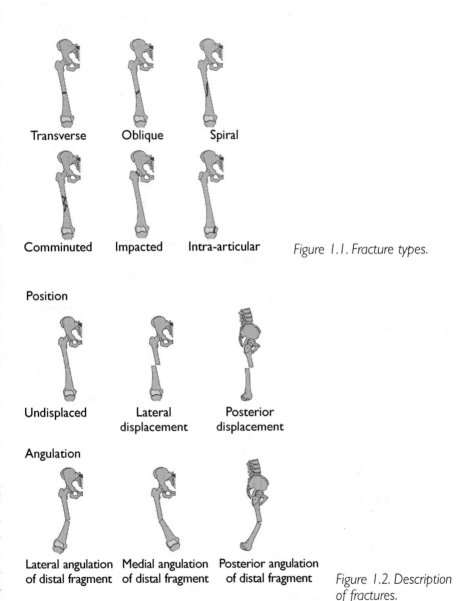

Transverse   Oblique   Spiral

Comminuted   Impacted   Intra-articular   *Figure 1.1. Fracture types.*

Position

Undisplaced   Lateral   Posterior
                displacement   displacement

Angulation

Lateral angulation   Medial angulation   Posterior angulation
of distal fragment   of distal fragment   of distal fragment   *Figure 1.2. Description of fractures.*

Basic principles of interpretation

Take a history and examine the patient before requesting films

A thorough assessment (full history and examination) of the patient is essential prior to requesting radiographs. Understanding the mechanism of injury allows relevant films to be taken and primes the doctor as to what to look for (*Figure 1.3*). In addition, since 2000, all radiological requests must be justified under IRMER (Ionizing Radiation Medical Exposure Regulations) legislation. This law aims to minimise exposure to ionising radiation whilst ensuing best practice, as followed by the Royal College of Radiologists' (2007) publication *Making the Best Use of Clinical Radiology Services*.

Treat the patient not the film

Life-threatening conditions such as shock and tension pneumothorax (*Figure 1.4*) need to be treated before a radiograph is taken. In some cases the radiograph will be normal but if an injury is suspected clinically then patients should be managed as if they had the condition, and imaging with other modalities (magnetic resonance or computed tomography in suspected fracture) or early follow up films arranged. Examples include scaphoid, wrist, hip and stress fractures that may be initially radiologically occult (*Figure 1.5*).

Know your anatomy and normal variants

There is no substitute for a good anatomical knowledge base when interpreting a radiograph, for example, knowing what structures are at risk of injury in a fracture of the first rib, a spiral fracture of the humerus and a chance fracture of the lumbar spine. In addition radiological anatomy must be understood as an axial view of the shoulder will be difficult to interpret if one does not know which is anterior and which posterior. There is also a wide spectrum of normal variants in adults, not to mention paediatric films (*Figure 1.6*). *Atlas of Normal Roentgen Variants that May Simulate Disease* (Keats and Anderson, 2006) is an essential reference book in any accident and emergency department. Ready access to a chart of normal skeletal development is also essential to ascertain the age of appearance and fusion of the epiphyses.

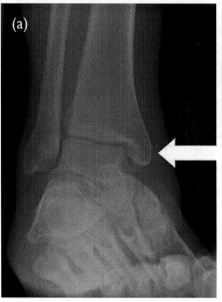

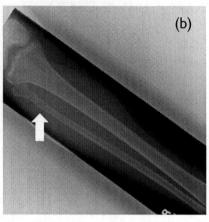

Figure 1.3. Maisonneuve fracture. (a) Shows a fracture of the medial malleolus. The patient gave a history of an external rotation injury which along with pain below the knee prompted film (b) to be performed. This showed an oblique fracture of the proximal fibula (arrow). The upper leg should be examined in all patients with an ankle injury to avoid missing this type of injury.

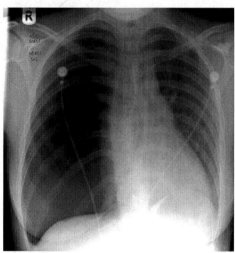

Figure 1.4. Right tension pneumothorax. The right hemidiaphragm is depressed inferiorly and the mediastinum is shifted to the left. This is a medical emergency and should have been diagnosed clinically and treated rather than endangering the patient by waiting to get a chest radiograph.

Check the films

Always obsessively check the patient's name, date of birth, side marker and quality of the radiograph. These also apply if you are asked to look at a film by a colleague. Make sure you have seen all the films in the packet. Do not

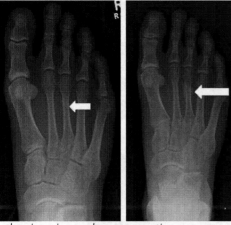

Figure 1.5. Stress fracture of the shaft of the 3rd metatarsal. The patient presented with pain in the absence of trauma. On the earlier film on the (left) there is subtle periosteal reaction (arrow) which was missed. The patient re-presented with increasing pain with an obvious fracture with callus (arrow) (right). Had the initial emergency doctor suspected a stress fracture from the history a follow up film or other imaging such as magnetic resonance or radionuclide imaging may have been arranged or it may even have been shown to a friendly radiologist.

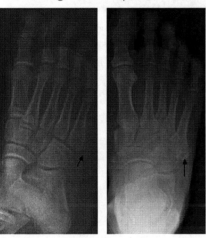

Figure 1.6. (left) Oblique view of a child's foot showing a normal unfused apophysis (arrow) at the base of the 5th metatarsal. The apophysis is parallel to the long axis of the metatarsal, while the fracture (right) is transverse (arrow).

be afraid to repeat the film if it is of poor quality, e.g poor inspiration chest radiograph or part of the bone omitted.

Look at the whole film

A systematic approach should be applied to the analysis of each film to avoid mistakes. The general systematic approach consists of film quality, alignment, bones, joints and soft tissues. The film should be viewed on a light box with bright light facilities for low density areas. A systematic approach will help avoid the 'switching' off phenomenon encountered after finding an abnormality, no matter how great or small (*Figure 1.7*). Remember to look all around a bone for fractures as well as at the four corners of the film.

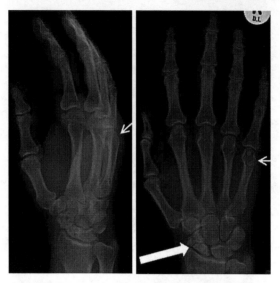

Figure 1.7. This patient presented with pain in the hand following a pub brawl. Little decipherable history was available. The two views show an old ununited fracture of the scaphoid with sclerosis of the proximal pole due to avascular necrosis (thick arrow) and an acute fracture of the neck of the 5th metacarpal (thin arrows). The message is not to switch off once one abnormality is found but to complete a systematic analysis of all the bones and soft tissues. In addition clinical acumen should be applied. The appearances of the scaphoid are consistent with an old injury and would not account for the acute presentation.

Two views

Suspected bony injury must be assessed using two views at right angles as the fracture may be visible on only one view (*Figures 1.8, 1.9*) and comments on displacement/angulation require at least two views. Additional views should be performed if there is a strong clinical suspicious of a particular injury, such as frog-leg views in slipped femoral capital epiphysis or shoot-through views of the shoulder in suspected dislocation. Comparison with old films is invaluable as the abnormality may have been present previously, albeit very subtly.

Try to minimise error

You should pay attention to red dots added to films by the radiographers as they are frequently more experienced than junior doctors in trauma films. However, the presence of a red dot does not mean there is a definite

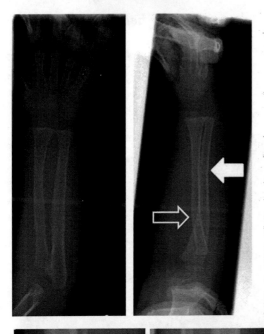

Figure 1.8. Forearm views of a child following trauma. The lateral film shows a torus fracture of the distal ulna (filled arrow) and a greenstick fracture of the proximal radius with angulation (open arrow).

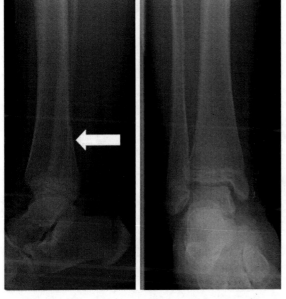

Figure 1.9. Oblique fracture (arrow) of the distal fibula seen on the lateral film that cannot be visualised on the anteroposterior (AP) view.

abnormality, merely a suspicion. It is still up to you to decide, or if you are still unsure show it to a colleague or radiologist.

All films should be formally reported by a radiologist and all errors audited and used in a constructive way to teach and train accident and emergency staff.

Know your limitations and when to ask for help

Avoid a headache (*Figure 1.10*). Do not be afraid to ask for a second opinion if you are unsure. Use the experience as a training exercise rather than an embarrassment. It may save you the embarrassment of a serious miss or a law suit.

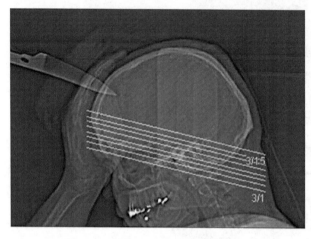

Figure 1.10. CT scanogram of a man stabbed in the head.

References

Keats TE, Anderson MW (2006) *Atlas of Normal Roentgen Variants that may Simulate Disease* (8th Edn). St Louis: Mosby

Royal College of Radiologists (2007) *Making the Best Use of Clinical Radiology Services* (6th Edn). London: Royal College of Radiologists

Chapter 2

Chest

Introduction

The chest X-ray (CXR) is the most common radiograph requested in casualty departments. However, all too often, relatively junior doctors, who have not been formally trained in interpretation of emergency radiographs, have to make instant decisions that profoundly affect patient management. In the space available here it is not possible to cover the numerous medical and surgical emergencies that may be encountered. This chapter provides a systematic approach to interpreting the chest film and describes the common emergency conditions requiring chest X-rays along with radiological signs.

Interpretaton of the chest radiograph

Technical factors

- **Posteroanterior** (PA) film: This chest radiograph is taken in the X-ray department. The X-ray tube is behind the patient and the cassette (or detector) against the anterior chest wall.
- **Anteroposterior** (AP) film: This is taken in the casualty setting when the patient is seriously ill, using a portable X-ray machine with the film cassette placed behind the patient. On an AP film the mediastinum appears falsely widened and there is apparent cardiomegaly, both findings due to the divergent direction of the X-ray beam. The AP film may have to be acquired in the supine position in which case the presence of upper lobe blood diversion is normal and pleural effusions may be missed as fluid tracks up the posterior chest wall.
- **Lateral** chest film: This may be useful to localise abnormalities on the frontal views.
- **Expiration** film: This may be useful to demonstrate a small pneumothorax.

Systematic radiological assessment

- The patient's name, date of birth and date on the film should always be checked.
- **Film quality**: The film projection should be checked (i.e. PA, AP, erect, supine). To assess for rotation, the medial ends of the clavicles should be equidistant from the spinous processes in a correctly centred film. To assess the degree of inspiration, the right hemidiaphragm should reach the anterior aspect of the sixth rib. A poor inspiration may simulate the appearance of basal collapse and cause spurious cardiomegaly.
- **Equipment**: The position of central lines, endotracheal (ET) tubes, chest drains, etc., should be noted. The tip of an ET tube should lie 3–5cm above the carina in adults.
- **Trachea:** This should normally be central. It may be deviated away from a superior mediastinal mass, e.g. thyroid goitre, or pulled by any process that causes volume loss, e.g. lung fibrosis.
- **Mediastinal contour:** The entire border of the heart and mediastinum should be clearly visualised. The constituents of the normal mediastinal contour should be recognised and assessed (*Figure 2.1*).
- **Heart:** The normal cardiothoracic ratio (ratio of transverse cardiac diameter to transverse inner thoracic diameter) is less than 50%. One third of the heart's diameter is positioned to the right and two thirds to the left of the spinous processes.
- **Hilar regions**: These are made up of the pulmonary arteries and veins (predominantly the upper lobe pulmonary vein and the lower lobe pulmonary artery). They have a concave lateral margin. They are of equal density and the right hilum is lower than the left.
- **Lungs**: These should be equal in density. When there is asymmetry, the side of decreased vascularity is usually the abnormal side. Inspect for focal lesions. The right horizontal fissure can be seen on frontal views whereas the oblique fissures are only usually visualised on lateral views.
- **Diaphragms**: On full inspiration the right hemidiaphragm is at the level of the 6th rib anteriorly and up to 3cm higher than the left hemidiaphragm in 95% of normal subjects. Inspect for free subdiaphragmatic gas due to perforation of a viscus (unless there is a known iatrogenic cause, such as a recent laparotomy or continuous ambulatory peritoneal dialysis). Also look for subphrenic abscesses, calcified liver lesions, gallstones and dilated bowel loops.
- **Review areas**: Check that both breasts are present, look for lesions behind the heart silhouette and lung apices, or at the hila. Check the bones for focal abnormalities, density and fractures. Check the shoulder

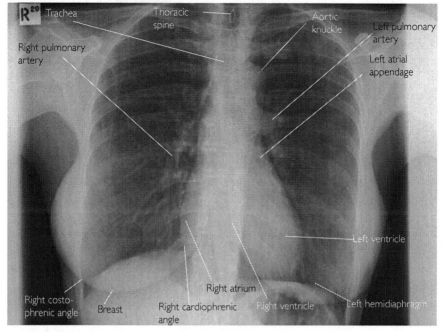

Figure 2.1. Normal PA chest radiograph with annotations.

joints if they are visible on the chest radiograph. Check the skin for surgical emphysema.

Rigorous radiological assessment may help to avoid common interpretative errors encountered in the emergency department (*Table 2.1*).

Table 2.1. Common interpretive errors

- Wrong patient/date
- Skin lesions/nipples/foreign bodies (buttons) mistaken for intrathoracic lesions
- Small apical pneumothoraces missed. Bullae/azygos lobe/skin folds/ medial edge of scapula mistaken for pneumothorax
- Apparent cardiomegaly due to pectus excavatum/scoliosis
- Pericardial cyst/fat pad mistaken for tumour
- Calcified costal cartilage or healing rib fracture mistaken for pleural or lung lesion
- Enlarged pulmonary arteries mistaken for tumour or lymphadenopathy
- Mastectomy commonly missed
- Costotransverse articulations mistaken for rib fracture
- Prominent vessels mistaken for mediastinal mass/nodes

Common emergencies

The common emergency conditions requiring chest X-rays can be divided into non-traumatic and traumatic causes.

Non-traumatic causes

Chest infection

On a conventional radiograph, four basic densities can be resolved: air, fat, soft tissues and calcification. An example of the value of natural contrast is the loss of silhouette sign. On a normal chest radiograph the heart and mediastinal interface is clearly visualised against the black lungs. However, in the presence of adjacent lung collapse or consolidation more X-rays are absorbed by the diseased lung, rendering it more opaque, and of similar X-ray attenuating density to the adjacent mediastinum, resulting in loss of the contour of adjacent structures (loss of the silhouette sign). An example of loss of the silhouette sign occurs in left lower lobe collapse: the medial aspect of the left hemidiaphragm and the lateral border of the lower descending thoracic aorta are lost because these structures now lie adjacent to collapsed left lower lobe which is denser than the alveolar air which would be present in the normal left lower lobe (*Figure 2.2*).

Table 2.2 lists radiological signs which may be present in collapse. Pure consolidation is denoted by the presence of opacification containing air bronchograms, no volume loss and obscuration of the normally visualised

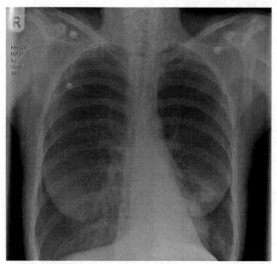

Figure 2.2. Left lower lobe collapse (arrows) seen as a wedge-shaped density posterior to the heart shadow. This is loss of the silhouette sign with obscuration of the medial aspect of the left hemidiaphragm. The left hilum is not seen as it has been pulled down with the lobar collapse. Note that the lungs are hyperinflated consistent with chronic obstructive pulmonary disease. The collapse was due to mucous plugging.

Table 2.2. Radiological features of collapse

On a CXR the basic features of lobar collapse are opacity and loss of volume. The resulting signs are:
- Increased density of pulmonary tissue
- Completely obscured pulmonary vessels
- Effacement of normally identified interfaces between air within the lung and surrounding soft tissues (silhouette sign)
- Displacement of fissures
- Displacement of the hilum towards the collapse
- Movement of bronchi and blood vessels (crowding in the affected lobe and splaying in the normal lobes on the same side)
- Elevation of the hemidiaphragm
- Shift of the mediastinum (heart and/or trachea) towards the side of collapse
- Compensatory hyperinflation of normal lung

pulmonary vessels (normally their soft tissue density contrasts against the air-filled lung). Air bronchograms are due to the presence of air-filled bronchi surrounded by pus-filled alveolar spaces. In practice, collapse and consolidation frequently coexist. The most common causes of collapse are pneumonia, mucous plugging (asthma), bronchial neoplasm and inhaled foreign body (*Figures 2.3, 2.4*). Clues to the site of the consolidation/collapse can be deduced by analysis

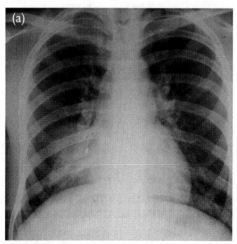 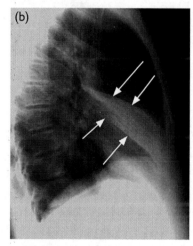

Figure 2.3. Right middle lobe collapse seen (a) on the frontal view as an opacity associated with loss of the right heart border (loss of the silhouette sign) and (b) on the lateral view as a wedge-shaped opacity. Reproduced with permission from Harvey et al. (1999) Radiology. A Casebook for MRCP. Oxford University Press.

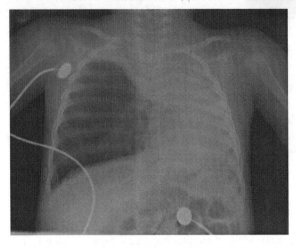

Figure 2.4. Complete collapse of the left lung, and right upper lobe collapse (arrow) due to erroneous position of an endotracheal tube in the bronchus intermedius. Reproduced with permission from Harvey et al. (2005) Self-Assessment Cases in Surgical Imaging. Oxford University Press.

Table 2.3. Radiological signs indicating the site of consolidation/collapse

Ill defined	Site of consolidation
Left heart border and aortic knuckle	Left upper lobe
Left hemidiaphragm and descending aorta	Left lower lobe
Right heart border	Right middle lobe
Right hemidiaphragm	Right lower lobe
Right superior mediastinum	Right upper lobe

of the film. If there is loss of clarity of a heart border or hemidiaphragm then collapse/consolidation in the adjacent lung is likely (*Table 2.3*).

Pulmonary embolism (PE)

The chest radiograph (CXR) is usually the first line of radiological investigation. There are a multitude of signs including subsegmental atelectasis (small volumes of collapse seen as linear densities), consolidation, infarction (classically wedged-shaped) and pleural effusion. These signs are non-specific. There are also some well-recognised signs including the Westermark sign (focal reduction in blood flow distal to an embolus resulting in increased translucency) and the Fleischner sign (dilatation of the pulmonary artery proximal to an embolus). However, in PE without infarction the CXR is normal in more than a third.

Table 2.4. Radiological signs of pulmonary oedema

- Upper lobe blood diversion
- Increased density over the lower zones of the lungs
- Peribronchial cuffing
- Perihilar airspace shadowing (bronchograms as a result of fluid in the alveolar spaces)
- Kerley's A and B lines (due to fluid in the interstitum causing thickening of the interlobular septa)

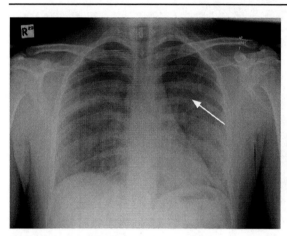

Figure 2.5. Acute left ventricular failure. There is bilateral perihilar airspace shadowing with bronchograms (arrow). Note the normal heart size in this case of pulmonary oedema associated with acute myocardial infarction.

Pulmonary oedema

Radiological signs (*Table 2.4, Figure 2.5*) usually precede clinical signs of cardiac failure. Cardiomegaly and pleural effusions may be present as part of cardiac failure.

Pleural effusion

On an erect CXR an effusion is seen as blunting of the costophrenic angle with basal opacification. The upper margin of this is concave to the lung and higher laterally (*Figure 2.6*). In contrast, the presence of a hydropneumothorax is denoted by a straight horizontal superior border of an effusion (*Figure 2.7*). There may be 200–500 ml present before this sign develops as fluid initially collects in the posterior costophrenic recess.

On the supine CXR there is reduced transradiancy due to dorsal pooling, with preserved lung vascular markings.

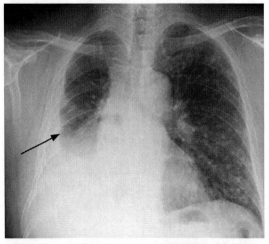

Figure 2.6. Right pleural effusion (arrow) with multiple pulmonary metastases seen in the left lung.

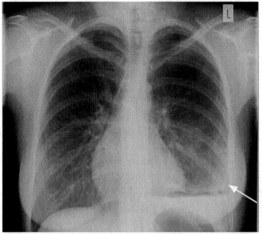

Figure 2.7. Left hydropneumothorax with a straight superior margin of the effusion. Note the basal pneumothorax (arrow).

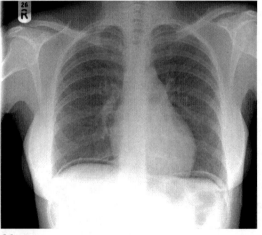

Figure 2.8. Pneumoperitoneum with free subdiaphragmatic gas bilaterally.

Abdominal pain

The erect CXR is very sensitive for the detection of pneumoperitoneum (*Figure 2.8*). Certain conditions may mimic pneumoperitoneum. These are Chilaiditi's syndrome (colon interposed between liver and diaphragm), subdiaphragmatic fat, subphrenic abscess, uneven diaphragm, pneumatosis coli and curvilinear basal collapse.

Inhaled foreign body

The foreign body may be seen if it is radiopaque. A lateral view may help to localise the lesion in the trachea or oesophagus. Typically, segmental or lobar collapse is seen. Acutely, air trapping may occur with hyperinflation and contralateral mediastinal shift due to a ball valve effect. See *Chapter 13* on foreign bodies for a more detailed discussion.

Aortic aneurysm

Radiological signs include mediastinal widening of greater than 8cm with an abnormal aortic contour (*Figure 2.9*). In aortic dissection other radiological features that may be present are tracheal or oesophageal displacement with calcification in the aortic knuckle which is separated

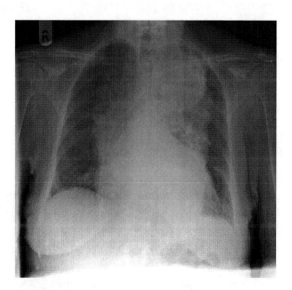

Figure 2.9. Large thoracic aortic aneurysm with gross mediastinal widening and abnormal aortic contour. The cardiomegaly was due to aortic regurgitation.

from the outer margin by more than 1cm. There may be cardiomegaly due to haemopericardium or aortic regurgitation. There may also be a pleural effusion or pleural apical cap. In traumatic aortic transection the CXR findings are indicators of the associated mediastinal haematoma. They include mediastinal widening, tracheal shift to the right, inferior displacement of the left main bronchus and widening of the paraspinal line without spinal fracture.

Trauma

Rib fracture

The role of the CXR in rib fracture is to exclude associated complications such as pneumothorax, and lung contusion. Oblique views of the ribs are unnecessary because management is seldom altered by demonstration of the fracture. In a flail segment (*Figure 2.10*) two or more ribs are fractured in two or more places. It is associated with major intrathoracic injury and may progress to respiratory failure.

Pneumothorax

Pneumothorax is best looked for on an erect expiratory film. The radiological signs are the presence of a lung edge and lack of lung markings peripheral to this edge. It is important not to confuse skin folds and bullae with pneumothoraces. The presence of contralateral mediastinal shift and ipsilateral diaphragmatic flattening/inversion is indicative of a tension pneumothorax which is a medical emergency (*Figure 2.11*). Surgical emphysema (*Figure 2.12*) and pneumomediastinum may be associated with pneumothoraces.

Diaphragmatic rupture

This may be caused by penetrating trauma or crush injury. It is more common on the left. Radiological signs include an ill-defined hemidiaphragmatic contour with herniation of bowel and organs into the thoracic cavity.

Pulmonary contusion

Radiologically this is seen as patchy airspace shadowing due to the presence of blood in the alveolar spaces. Associated injuries such as pneumothorax, cardiac contusion and fractures should be sought.

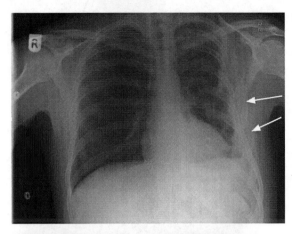

Figure 2.10. Flail segment of the left chest wall with multiple ribs fractured in two or more sites (arrows) following a road traffic accident.

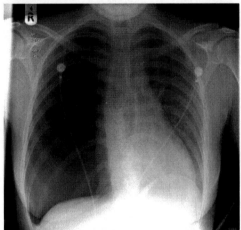

Figure 2.11. Tension pneumothorax with mediastinal shift to the left. Reproduced with permission from Harvey et al. (2005) Self-Assessment Cases in Surgical Imaging. Oxford University Press.

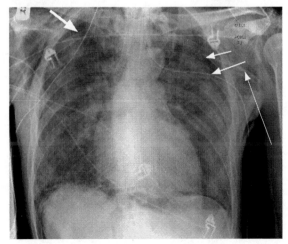

Figure 2.12. Adult respiratory distress syndrome (ARDS) with bilateral airspace shadowing consistent with pulmonary oedema, bilateral pneumothoraces (thick arrows) and surgical emphysema (thin arrow).

Penetrating chest trauma

Check for pneumothorax, pneumoperitoneum, cardiac tamponade (globular cardiomegaly), transected aorta, ruptured diaphragm and major airway injury.

Key points

- Always check the patient's name and age and date of the film
- Assess film quality
- Check the mediastinal contour and hilar regions
- Check the diaphragms and subdiaphragmatic areas
- Inspect the lungs, paying particular attention to the apices and behind the heart
- Note the presence of medical equipment
- Check the bones and extrathoracic soft tissues

CHAPTER 3

Abdomen

Introduction

Abdominal symptoms are a common presenting complaint in casualty departments and constitute a significant percentage of emergencies. The abdominal radiograph is still the commonest initial imaging investigation to exclude obstruction or perforation. Since many conditions may present with abdominal pain a rigorous analysis of the abdominal radiograph is essential to avoid missing important diagnostic radiological signs. This chapter provides a systematic approach to interpreting the abdominal film and describes the common emergency conditions requiring abdominal radiographs along with radiological signs.

Interpretation of the abdominal radiograph

Technical factors

- **Supine film**: This is the standard view. The erect chest radiograph (CXR) is an integral part of the assessment of the acute abdomen as it is the most sensitive radiograph for the detection of pneumoperitoneum. An erect abdominal film is hardly ever performed as it seldom adds further diagnostic information to the supine abdomen and erect chest films.

Systematic radiological assessment

- The patient's name, date of birth and date on the film should always be checked.
- **Film quality**: The supine abdominal radiograph should include from the diaphragms to the hernial orifices.
      The normal abdominal radiograph has a wide variation in normal appearances. The properitoneal line (flank stripe) extends from the lateral liver margin to just below the iliac crest. It is due to the presence of a thin layer of extraperitoneal fat between the parietal

peritoneum and the inner muscle layer (transversalis). The ascending and descending colon is seen in the flanks adjacent to the properitoneal stripes (*Figure 3.1*).

- **Calcifications:** Inspect for renal tract calculi (90% are radio-opaque), gallstones (10–15% are radio-opaque), pancreatic calcification (*Figure 3.2*), appendoliths and calcified aortic aneurysms. Renal tract calcification may be due to calculi, nephrocalcinosis, prostatic calcification, tuberculosis (TB) and tumours. Most calcifications are not significant (phleboliths, lymph nodes, arterial walls, fibroids and costal cartilage).

- **Bowel gas pattern**: Gas is normally seen in the stomach (seen as characteristic gastric rugae) and colon. There are a number of features that can be used to distinguish small from large bowel (*Table 3.1*). Small amounts of air may be seen in the small bowel which can be distinguished from colon by the presence of valvulae conniventes which cross the whole small bowel loop. Haustral folds of the colon are usually seen extending only across part of the large bowel lumen and are thicker and further apart than valvulae conniventes. Small bowel loops should not exceed 2.5–3.0cm in diameter. The colonic calibre is variable but is dilated when the diameter is greater than 5cm and the caecum when it exceeds 8cm. Dilatation of the bowel occurs in obstruction, paralytic ileus, ischaemia and inflammatory bowel disease. Look for intramural gas. Linear intramural gas is seen in ischaemic bowel whereas cystic intramural gas is a feature of the benign condition pneumatosis intestinalis.

- **Ectopic gas**: look for pneumobilia, portal venous gas and gas in the genitourinary tract. Gas may be seen in the gallbladder and urinary bladder in diabetes mellitus due to emphysematous infections.

Table 3.1. Distinguishing features of the small and large bowel

	Small Bowel	Large Bowel
Haustra	Absent	Present (may be absent sigmoid)
Valvulae conniventes	Present (jejunum)	Absent
Number of loops	Many	Few
Distribution of loops	Central	Peripheral
Radius of curvature	Small	Large
Diameter of loop	2.5–3.0 cm	>5cm
Solid faeces	Absent	Present

- **Viscera**: the liver, spleen, kidneys and psoas silhouettes may normally be seen as they are silhouetted by fat. Retroperitoneal pathology will result in loss of the psoas silhouette (*Figure 3.3*)
- **Pelvic masses:** may be due to the bladder or gynaecological lesions.
- **Bones**: The lower ribs, lumbar spine and pelvis should be inspected for focal lesions and injury. If fractures are present associated visceral injury to the liver, spleen and kidneys should be excluded.

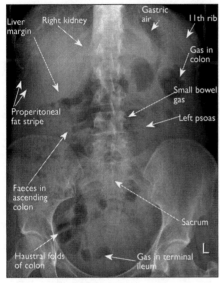

Figure 3.1. Normal abdominal radiograph with annotations.

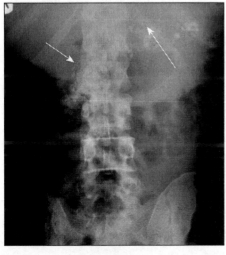

Figure 3.2. Pancreatic calcification (arrows) is present consistent with chronic pancreatitis. Reproduced with permission from Harvey et al. (1999) Radiology. A Casebook for MRCP. Oxford University Press.

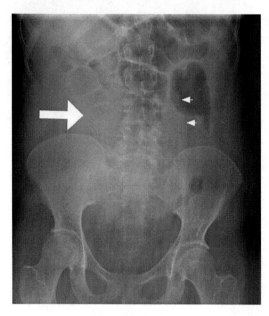

Figure 3.3. There is loss of the normal right psoas outline with an area of increased density over the right flank (arrow) due to retroperitoneal haemorrhage in a patient with haemophilia. The normal left psoas silhouette can be seen (arrowheads). Reproduced with permission from Harvey et al. (2005) Self-Assessment Cases in Surgical Imaging. Oxford University Press.

Rigorous radiological assessment may help to avoid common interpretative errors encountered in casualty (*Table 3.2*).

Table 3.2. Common interpretive errors

- Wrong patient/date
- Erroneous diagnosis of pnemoperitoneum. Conditions which mimic pneumoperitoneum include Chilaiditi syndrome (interposition of colon between the liver and diaphragm), subphrenic abscess, subdiaphragmatic fat, basal curvilinear atelectasis, uneven diaphragm, distended abdominal viscus, subpulmonic pneumothorax and cysts in pneumatosis coli
- Mistaking pelvic phleboliths for ureteric stones. Phleboliths have a central lucency surrounded by a radio-opaque halo
- Skin lesions/foreign bodies (buttons) mistaken for abdominal lesions
- The properitoneal line may be mistaken for a pneumoperitoneum especially in the decubitus position
- Calcified costal cartilage or healing rib fracture mistaken for liver lesions, gallstones or renal calculi

Pneumoperitoneum

The erect chest radiograph (CXR) is the most sensitive radiograph for the detection of pneumoperitoneum (*Figure 3.4*). Of all perforations, 70–90% show detectable free gas. As little as 1 ml of free gas can be detected but the patient should remain in position for 5–10 minutes prior to taking the radiograph to allow any air to rise. If the patient is too ill to allow an erect CXR to be performed then a left lateral decubitus radiograph can be substituted to look for a pneumoperitoneum (*Figure 3.5a, b*). Alternatively a CT may be performed which is extremely sensitive in the detection of

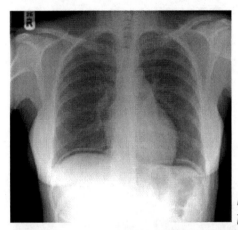

Figure 3.4. Pneumoperitoneum with free subdiaphragmatic gas bilaterally.

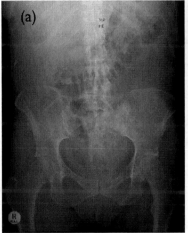

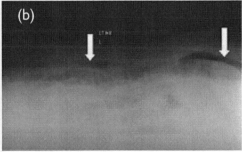

Figure 3.5. 68-year-old lady admitted with severe epigastric pain. (a) The supine abdominal radiograph is unremarkable. (b) As there was a high index of suspicion for a perforated viscus a left lateral decubitus film was performed which revealed free intraperitoneal gas lateral to the liver and in the flank (arrows). A perforated duodenal ulcer was found at laparotomy. Courtesy of Dr William Partridge.

Table 3.3. Signs of free intraperitoneal gas on the supine radiograph

- Rigler's sign: Air outlining both sides of the bowel wall (*Figure 3.6*). This usually requires more than a litre of gas
- Air outlining the falciform ligament (*Figure 3.6*)
- Inverted 'V' sign: Air outlining the umbilical ligaments
- Lateral flank sign: Air interposed between the colon and properitoneal fat stripe
- Football sign: A central collection of gas anterior to loops of bowel
- 50% of patients with free gas will have a collection of air adjacent to the liver lying in the subhepatic space, parahepatic (gas lateral to right edge of liver) and hepatorenal space (Morison's pouch)
- Triangular-shaped gas collections are suspicious of free gas as they do not conform to normal bowel gas patterns
- Urachus sign: Air outlining the middle umbilical ligament
- Cupola or saddlebag sign: Gas trapped below the central tendon of diaphragm

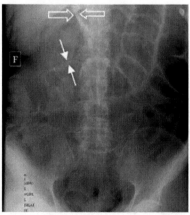

Figure 3.6. Pneumoperitoneum due to biopsy induced perforation of the sigmoid colon. There is free intraperitoneal gas throughout the abdomen seen as gas either side of the large (arrows) and small bowel wall (Rigler's sign). The falciform ligament (open arrows) is outlined by gas. There is also free gas (F) in the subhepatic space outlining the gallbladder and liver. Reproduced with permission from Harvey et al. (2005) Self-Assessment Cases in Surgical Imaging. Oxford University Press.

free intra-peritoneal gas and may demonstrate the underlying cause, e.g. perforated colon cancer. However, it is still important to recognise the signs of free intraperitoneal gas on the supine film as the patient may be too ill to obtain other films (*Table 3.3*) (*Figure 3.6*). In about 56% of patients with a pneumoperitoneum the gas may be detectable on a supine film. Approximately 60% of all post-laparotomy patients have evidence of a pneumoperitoneum and this may take up to 24 days to be reabsorbed, depending on body habitus. However, in the majority of cases the free gas is reabsorbed by 72 hours. In the obese patient the gas is more rapidly absorbed and normally there is no residual gas after the fourth post-operative day. An increase in gas post-operatively may indicate an anastomotic leak or perforation.

Bowel obstruction

Dilatation of the bowel is the hallmark of obstruction but also occurs in obstruction, paralytic ileus, ischaemia and inflammatory bowel disease.

Small bowel obstruction

Small bowel loops are considered dilated when they exceed 3cm in diameter and has a number of causes (*Table 3.4*) (*Figure 3.7*). The radiological features of small bowel obstruction include:

- Multiple central dilated central small bowel loops 3–5 hours after the onset of obstruction.
- 'Stepladder appearance' in low small bowel obstruction.
- Sparse/absent colonic gas in complete small bowel obstruction after 12–24 hours.
- Multiple fluid levels on the erect film. This is a non-specific sign occurring in a number of conditions such as ileus, gastroenteritis and ischaemia.
- 'String of beads' sign (virtually pathognomonic): This sign is seen on the erect film and occurs when dilated small bowel loops are almost completely full of fluid and small gas bubbles become trapped between the valvulae conniventes.
- Stretch sign: The valvulae conniventes completely encircle the bowel lumen.

Table 3.4. Causes of small bowel obstruction in adults

- Adhesions: 49%
- Hernia: 21% (the hernial orifices must be inspected on the film for evidence of soft tissue masses)
- Gallstone ileus
- Intussusception
- Tumour
- Volvulus

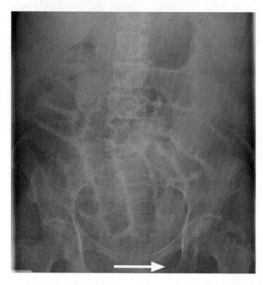

Figure 3.7. There is small bowel obstruction secondary to a strangulated left inguinal hernia (arrow). No gas is seen in the large bowel.

When the bowel loops are completely fluid filled obstruction may be missed. Proximal small bowel obstruction may present in this way.

Large bowel obstruction

The colonic calibre is variable but is dilated when the diameter is greater than 5cm and the caecum when it exceeds 8cm. The commonest cause of large bowel obstruction is carcinoma (*Table 3.5*) (*Figure 3.8*). In the presence of a competent ileocaecal valve colonic dilatation alone occurs with risk of caecal perforation when greater than 10cm in diameter. When the ileocaecal valve is incompetent the small bowel also becomes dilated.

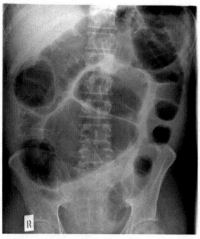

Figure 3.8. There is large bowel obstruction secondary to a distal sigmoid carcinoma. The caecum is markedly dilated and at risk of perforation. There is only a small amount of gas in the small bowel indicating a competent ileocaecal valve.

Table 3.5. Causes of large bowel obstruction in adults

- Carcinoma (sigmoid or rectosigmoid)
- Diverticular disease
- Volvulus

Pseudo-obstruction

This is a functional disorder that mimics obstruction but no obstructing lesion is present. Causes include electrolyte imbalance, sepsis, drugs, intra-abdominal inflammation, autonomic neuropathy and cardiac failure. A true organic obstruction must be excluded, usually by a contrast enema. Perforation may be a complication of this condition.

Ileus

This is a stasis of bowel due to a functional abnormality of peristalsis (decreased or absent) with failure of distal propulsion of intestinal contents. An ileus may be localised or generalised. A localised ileus is seen as a persistent dilated segment of bowel adjacent to a focal inflammatory process such as pancreatitis or pyelonephritis. There are a large number of causes (*Table 3.6*). The degree of dilatation may vary considerably and when generalised cannot be distinguished radiologically from a low large bowel obstruction. The clinical features usually allow differentiation.

Table 3.6. Causes of ileus

- Pancreatitis
- Appendicitis
- Peptic ulcer
- Perforation
- Postoperative
- Peritonitis
- Potassium deficiency
- Pyelonephritis

Volvulus

Volvulus accounts for approximately 10% of cases of large bowel obstruction. Volvulus occurs where the mesentery is longest allowing that segment to twist. The commonest site is the sigmoid, followed by the caecum.

Sigmoid volvulus is common in African and Asian countries due to the population's high fibre diet. In the West patients are commonly elderly, or psychiatric cases. The sigmoid becomes a greatly distended, paralysed ahaustral loop and this has the appearance of a 'coffee bean' on the supine radiograph (*Figure 3.9*). It arises from the left side of the pelvis and extends superiorly to the right side of the abdomen.

Caecal volvulus occurs in a younger age group, 20–40 years. In about 50% of patients, the caecum twists and inverts so that the caecum is sited in the left upper quadrant. In the other 50% the caecum twists in the axial plane without inversion so that the caecum remains in the right lower quadrant (*Figure 3.10*). On the abdominal radiograph the volvulus appears as a 'kidney shaped' distension of the caecum. There are usually a few haustral markings compared to a complete absence in sigmoid volvulus. Small bowel obstruction is often associated with collapse of the left colon.

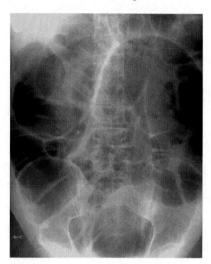

Figure 3.9. There is a markedly distended loop of bowel arising from the pelvis and extending to the left upper quadrant. The loop has the appearance of a coffee bean. There are no haustral markings of the bowel loop. Appearances are consistent with a sigmoid volvulus with proximal large bowel obstruction. Reproduced with permission from Harvey et al. (2005) Self-Assessment Cases in Surgical Imaging. Oxford University Press.

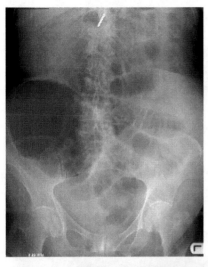

Figure 3.10. There is a large dilated loop of bowel with thickened wall in the right iliac fossa consistent with a caecal volvulus. There is associated small bowel obstruction but no large bowel dilatation. Reproduced with permission from Harvey et al. (2005) Self-Assessment Cases in Surgical Imaging. Oxford University Press.

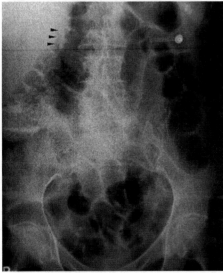

Figure 3.11. Gallstone ileus. There is aerobilia (arrows), small bowel obstruction and multiple radio-opaque gallstones in the gallbladder. Pelvic densities are present, one of which is the impacted stone at the ileocaecal valve. Reproduced with permission from Harvey et al. (1999) Radiology. A Casebook for MRCP. Oxford University Press.

Gallstone ileus

Gallstone ileus (*Figure 3.11*) is an uncommon cause of small bowel obstruction (about 1%) but has a high mortality. However, with increasing age it becomes a more likely cause of intestinal obstruction (25% in patients over 70 years). The gallstone enters the small bowel via a fistula. This is most commonly cholecystoduodenal (60%) and results in aerobilia seen as a branching lucencies arising from the liver hilum in contrast to the peripheral air present with portal venous gas. The gallstone needs to be larger than 2.5

cm to cause small bowel obstruction. The gallstone most commonly impacts in the terminal ileum (60–70%).

The classic plain radiograph triad (Rigler's triad) is: intestinal obstruction (80%), gas in the biliary tree (70%) and an ectopic calcified gallstone (25%).

Intussusception

Intussusception is one of the most common abdominal emergencies of early childhood (*Figure 3.12*). It is most commonly ileocolic (75–95%) in children compared with ileo-ileal (40%) in adults. The aetiology is idiopathic in over 95% in children and is thought to be due to lymphoid hyperplasia of Peyer's patches. In adults 80% have a specific cause, including benign neoplasm (one third), malignant neoplasm (one fifth), Meckel's diverticulum, foreign body and trauma.

The diagnosis often requires a high level of suspicion. The plain radiograph is normal in 25% but shows an abdominal soft tissue mass in 50% (commonly in the right upper quadrant). Small bowel obstruction is present in 25%.

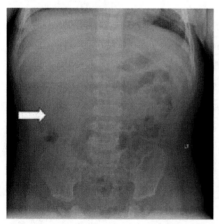

Figure 3.12. Intussusception in a 15-month-old boy. There is a soft tissue mass surrounded by a thin crescent of air just inferior to the liver (arrow) consistent with an intussuscepted caecum/ascending colon. Note the absence of bowel gas in the right iliac fossa. There is no free intraperitoneal gas or evidence of small bowel obstruction.

Acute colitis

The abdominal radiograph can be used to assess the extent of mucosal involvement in acute colitis. The disease in unlikely to be active where there are formed faeces. The depth of ulceration, perforation and presence of toxic megacolon (*Figure 3.13*) can all be made on plain film. Toxic megacolon is due to transmural fulminant colitis with neuromuscular degeneration. This results in rapid colon dilatation (>5.5cm is abnormal). Typically

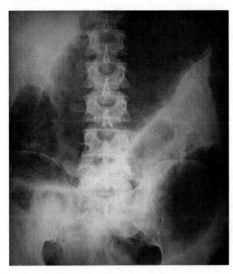

Figure 3.13. Toxic megacolon. The transverse colon is grossly dilated at 12cm with thickening of the bowel wall. Mucosal islands (pseudopolyps) are present which represent areas of normal mucosa. Reproduced with permission from Harvey et al. (1999) Radiology. A Casebook for MRCP. Oxford University Press.

there is loss of the normal haustral pattern with bowel wall thickening and pseudopolyposis (mucosal islands in denuded ulcerated colonic wall). It is important to differentiate toxic megacolon from other causes of a dilated colon where the mucosal pattern will be normal, e.g. ileus, pseudo-obstruction and true obstruction. As well as the radiological findings, the diagnosis is also based on the patient's clinical condition, i.e. the presence of pyrexia, tachycardia and leucocytosis. Perforation and ensuing peritonitis may occur with a high mortality (>20%). Perforation may be heralded by linear air within the bowel wall.

Ischaemic colitis

Ischaemic colitis most commonly affects the splenic flexure and descending colon. Radiologically it is characterised by bowel wall thickening (described as thumbprinting due to bowel wall oedema and haemorrhage). A functional obstruction occurs with proximal colonic dilatation. The development of linear intramural gas heralds necrosis which may be followed by perforation. Portal venous gas is a poor prognostic sign.

Trauma

Plain radiography is rarely indicated when investigating blunt or penetrating injury. Computed tomography (CT) is the most useful modality in the assessment of abdominal injury if the patient is haemodynamically stable and does not require urgent laparotomy. However, often the abdominal

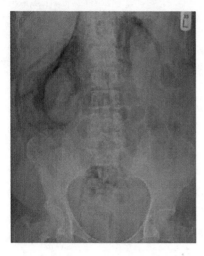

Figure 3.14. Retroperitoneal gas outlining the kidneys secondary to a ruptured third part of duodenum.

radiograph is used as the first investigation in the initial assessment while waiting for other imaging. Liver and splenic injury should be suspected in lower rib fractures. The gastric air bubble may be displaced medially by a splenic haematoma. Bleeding into the paracolic gutters will result in widening of the space between the ascending or descending colon and the properitoneal flank stripe. Intestinal injury may manifest as free intraperitoneal gas or retroperitoneal gas in rupture of the third part of duodenum (*Figure 3.14*). Abdominal radiographs may be useful in identifying shrapnel and foreign bodies.

Renal colic

Ninety percent of all renal tract calculi are radio-opaque (*Figure 3.15*). They need to be distinguished from pelvic phleboliths which have a lucent centre and a smooth spherical contour. A plain film is usually performed as part of an intravenous urogram (IVU) to exclude obstruction. Complications of an obstruction such as a urinoma or emphysematous pyelonephritis (*Figure 3.16*) can be diagnosed on plain films. A urinoma is due to a rupture of the pelvicalyceal system resulting in a retroperitoneal collection of urine and may be suspected on plain film in the presence of a soft tissue mass obscuring the renal and psoas contours. It is usually confirmed by IVU. Emphysematous pyelonephritis and emphysematous cystitis, which are more common in diabetics, are seen as linear gas tracts in the renal tubules and bladder wall. CT will largely replace the conventional IVU over the next few years because it is more sensitive than radiography and ultrasound in the detection of

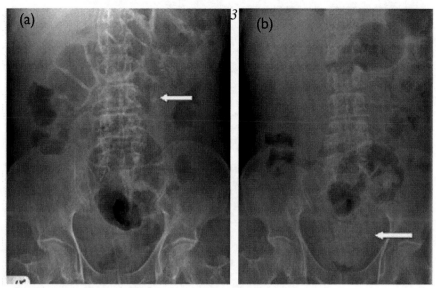

Figure 3.15. Left ureteric stone.
(a) There is a 1cm stone at the left pelvicalyceal junction (arrow).
(b) On a follow-up film the stone has passed distally and impacted at the left ureterovesical junction (UVJ) (arrow) causing obstruction.

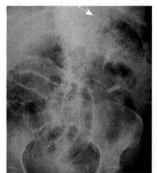

Figure 3.16. Emphysematous pyelonephritis. Streaks of gas are seen in the renal parenchyma radiating from the medulla to the cortex (arrow). There is also an associated small bowel ileus. Reproduced with permission from Harvey et al. (1999) Radiology. A Casebook for MRCP. *Oxford University Press.*

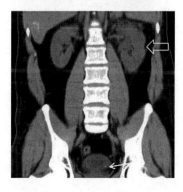

Figure 3.17. Coronal reformat from a CT which shows hydronephrosis of the left kidney (open arrow) due to an obstructing 6mm stone (arrow) at the vesico-ureteric junction that was radiolucent and therefore not visualised on plain film (not shown).

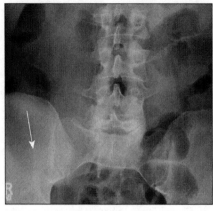

Figure 3.18. Acute appendicitis. There is a calcified appendolith (arrow) in the right iliac fossa with an associated small bowel ileus. Reproduced with permission from Harvey et al. (2005) Self-Assessment Cases in Surgical Imaging. Oxford University Press.

Acute appendicitis

There are no specific radiological signs of acute appendicitis. The combination of an appendolith and right iliac fossa pain equates with a 90% probability of acute appendicitis (*Figure 3.18*). Plain film signs include:

- Calcified appendolith 7-15%.
- Caecal ileus (sentinel loop) (gas fluid level in gangrene).
- Small bowel ileus. Obstruction may occur associated with an abscess.
- Blurring and widening of the properitoneal flank stripe.
- Extraluminal gas (in 33% of perforations). Pneumoperitoneum and pneumoretroperitoneum are rare.
- Colon cut-off sign (amputation of gas at the hepatic flexure) due to spastic ascending colon.
- Gas in the appendix. This is unreliable and may be seen in normals, ileus and large bowel obstruction.
- Scoliosis concave to the right.

Acute cholecystitis

Only one third of films show any abnormality. Signs include:

- Gallstones – radio-opaque in 10%.
- Pneumobilia (however this sign has many causes).
- Duodenal or hepatic flexure ileus.
- Right hypochondrial mass due to distended gallbladder.

The diagnosis is best made by ultrasound.

Acute pancreatitis

A large number of signs have been described on plain radiography, most of which are of little use in the diagnosis of this condition. These include:

- Rare but diagnostic:
  - Gas in the pancreas.
- Common and sometimes helpful:
  - Atonic stomach/duodenum.
  - Small bowel ileus.
  - Sentinel loop.
  - Loss of left psoas outline.
  - Dilated colon.
- Uncommon and unhelpful:
  - Pancreatic calcification.
  - Radio-opaque gallstones.
  - Pleural effusion/basal atelectasis/elevated hemidiaphragm.
  - Loss of right psoas outline.

Key points

- Always check the patient's name and age and date of the film
- Assess film quality. The supine abdominal radiograph should include from the diaphragms to the hernial orifices
- Check for free intraperitoneal gas on erect CXR, supine abdominal film and lateral decubitus view if necessary
- Analyse the bowel gas pattern. This must always be done with full knowledge of the clinical presentation. Does the bowel gas pattern equate with obstruction, ileus, pseudo-obstruction, ischaemia or inflammatory bowel disease?
- Look for abnormal calcification
- Look for ectopic gas
- Major trauma is best assessed by CT
- Check the bones and extrathoracic soft tissues

CHAPTER 4

Shoulder

Introduction

What the shoulder has gained in manoeuvrability has been at the expense of strength and stability. More than other joints the shoulder relies on dynamic stabilisation by coordinated muscle groups and is vulnerable to relatively low impact trauma. The tendency to use the arms protectively in a fall also means that excessive forces may be transmitted through the shoulder girdle and lead to fractures.

The patient's history is important in determining the mechanism of injury and most fractures or dislocations will be apparent on clinical examination. Conventional (X-ray) radiography provides the mainstay of traumatic shoulder imaging and it is important to request the appropriate views to avoid misinterpretation. Computed tomography (CT) may be used as a second-line investigation in complex fractures that require surgical intervention. It is important to remember that musculotendinous and cartilaginous injuries may not be apparent on plain radiographs and that ultrasound and magnetic resonance imaging (MRI) may be used to image these structures in selected cases.

Anatomy

The shoulder girdle consists of the clavicle, scapula and humerus. The synovial sternoclavicular joint articulates with the manubrium and the first costal cartilage. It permits limited rotatory movement of the clavicle. Its fibrous capsule is further reinforced by the costoclavicular and sternoclavicular ligaments. The clavicle acts as a strut between the upper limb and the trunk, and provides attachments for the deltoid, trapezius and pectoralis major muscles. The subclavian vessels and the brachial plexus pass between the clavicle and the first rib.

The acromioclavicular joint is a plane synovial joint which articulates with the acromion process of the scapula. Its weak fibrous capsule is strengthened by the acromioclavicular ligament, with the coracoclavicular ligaments providing vertical stability.

The triangular scapula lies over the posterior costal surfaces. It has three bony eminences: the spine and acromion, the coracoid process and the glenoid.

It articulates with the clavicle and the humerus. The shallow glenoid fossa is deepened by a fibrocartilaginous labrum which accepts part of the humeral head to form the ball-and-socket glenohumeral joint. The superior portion of the labrum blends with the tendon of the long head of the biceps brachii muscle. The surrounding capsule is loose to allow a full range of movement. The joint is strengthened by the glenohumeral, coracohumeral, transverse humeral and coraco-acromial ligaments. Dynamic stability is provided by the rotator cuff complex which passes from the scapular surfaces to insert on to the lesser and greater tubercles of the humerus.

The anatomical neck of the humerus separates the head from the tubercles and is where the joint capsule is attached. Just below this level is the surgical neck which is prone to fracturing.

Radiographic views

The anteroposterior (AP) view is the primary projection for evaluating the shoulder (*Figure 4.1*). The humeral head is asymmetrical and typically has an appearance similar to the head of a walking stick. The articular surfaces of the humeral head and the glenoid fossa should be parallel to each other. The fused humeral growth plate may appear as two wavy lines passing between the tubercles and should not be mistaken for fractures. The unfused ossification centres of the acromion and coracoid have a typical location and an intact cortex. The undersurface of the acromion and the distal clavicle should form a straight line and the joint space should not exceed 10mm.

In order to assess the alignment of the glenohumeral joint an axial view is performed with the patient abducting the arm (*Figure 4.2a, b*). The humeral head should be seen to articulate with the glenoid fossa. The acromion process and coracoid are directed anteriorly on this projection. If the patient's

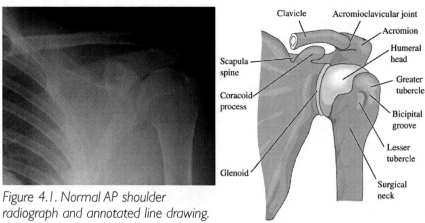

Figure 4.1. Normal AP shoulder radiograph and annotated line drawing.

movements are limited by pain then a lateral scapular or Y-view may be performed (*Figure 4.3a, b*). In this view the humeral head is projected over the glenoid, and the acromion and coracoid lie on either side forming a Y-shape.

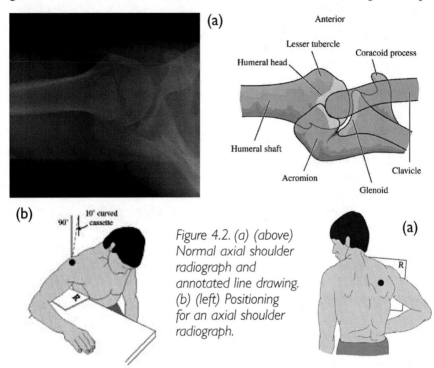

(a)

Anterior

Lesser tubercle

Humeral head

Coracoid process

Humeral shaft

Acromion

Clavicle

Glenoid

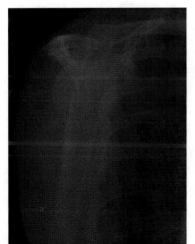

(b)

90° 10° curved cassette

Figure 4.2. (a) (above) Normal axial shoulder radiograph and annotated line drawing. (b) (left) Positioning for an axial shoulder radiograph.

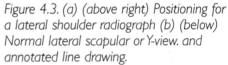

(a)

R

Figure 4.3. (a) (above right) Positioning for a lateral shoulder radiograph (b) (below) Normal lateral scapular or Y-view. and annotated line drawing.

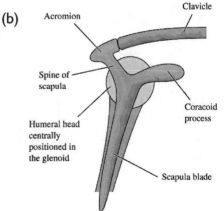

(b)

Clavicle

Acromion

Spine of scapula

Humeral head centrally positioned in the glenoid

Coracoid process

Scapula blade

Table 4.1. Common interpretive errors

- Missing a posterior shoulder dislocation
- Not looking for a Bankart or Hill-Sacks fracture
- Incorrect understanding of anatomy on axial view
- Overlooking impacted fractures

Common errors of interpretation are shown in *Table 4.1*.

Shoulder injuries

Proximal humeral fractures

Fractures of the proximal humerus usually involve the surgical neck. They are considered displaced if the fragments are separated by more than 10mm or the angulation exceeds 45 degrees (*Figure 4.4*). More complex fractures involve the humeral head, and the lesser and greater tubercles (*Figure 4.5*), and may be associated with avascular necrosis. These injuries are often seen in the elderly following a fall and may be associated with shoulder dislocation and injuries to the wrist and hip.

Acromioclavicular joint injuries

Injury to the acromioclavicular joint is usually as a result of direct trauma. In severe injuries the fibrous capsule and coracoclavicular ligaments are

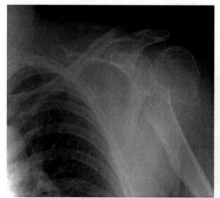

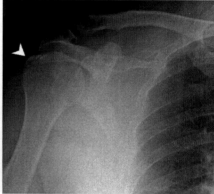

Figure 4.4. A displaced fracture of the surgical neck of the humerus.

Figure 4.5. A fracture of the greater tubercle of the humerus (arrow).

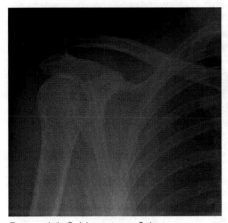

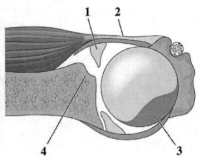

Figure 4.7. Consequences of recurrent shoulder dislocation. (1) Bankart lesion. (2) Atrophy of the rotator cuff (3) Hill-Sacks lesion. (4) Flattening of the glenoid fossa.

Figure 4.6. Subluxation of the acromioclavicular joint.

disrupted causing joint instability. The distal end of the clavicle is superiorly subluxed and its undersurface forms a step where it meets the acromion process (*Figure 4.6*). Less severe sprains may not be apparent unless the joint is put under stress by holding a weight in the hand while the radiograph is taken. Comparison views with the asymptomatic side may be useful as there is a range of normal appearances. Non-traumatic pathology, such as rheumatoid arthritis or hyperparathyroidism, may cause erosion of the distal end of the clavicle and give the appearance of a widened acromioclavicular joint space.

Glenohumeral joint

The shoulder joint has a wide range of movement but is relatively unstable and prone to dislocation. The vast majority of dislocations are anterior as a result of external rotation and abduction. As a consequence the humeral head comes to lie in a subcoracoid location. During the process of dislocation a compression fracture of the posterolateral humeral head may occur (Hill-Sachs deformity), or the anterior bony glenoid or its fibrocartilaginous labrum may be fractured (Bankart lesion) (*Figure 4.7*). In 10% of anterior dislocations there is an associated fracture of the greater tubercle. Anterior dislocations are usually readily apparent with the humeral head lying below the coracoid process on the AP view (*Figure 4.8*), and anterior to the glenoid on the axial or Y-views (*Figure 4.9*). It is important to obtain post-reduction radiographs to document the joint alignment and to scrutinise the film for associated fractures.

Posterior dislocations are much rarer and are less easy to appreciate both clinically and radiographically. They are usually associated with seizures or

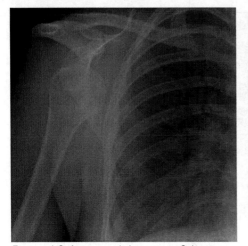

Figure 4.8. Anterior dislocation of the humeral head (AP view). The humerus lies in a sub-coracoid position.

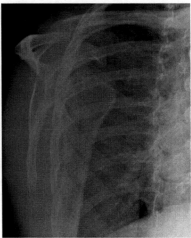

Figure 4.9. Anterior dislocation of the humeral head (lateral scapular or Y-view). The humeral head is displaced anteriorly revealing the glenoid fossa.

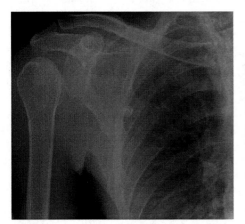

Figure 4.10. Posterior dislocation of the humeral head (AP view). The humeral head has a 'light bulb' appearance due to internal rotation of the shoulder. The glenohumeral joint space is widened.

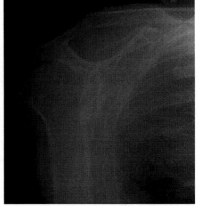

Figure 4.11. Posterior dislocation of the humeral head (lateral scapular or Y-view). The humeral head is displaced posteriorly below the acromion process.

electrocutions, but may result from severe trauma. Forced posterior movement and internal rotation cause the humeral head to rest under the acromion process. On the AP view the internal rotation of the humeral head may give it a characteristic 'light bulb' appearance (*Figure 4.10*). The glenohumeral joint space also appears widened and there may be decreased overlap of the

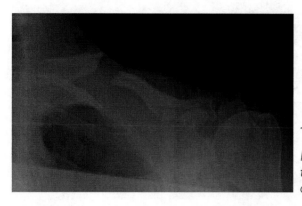

Figure 4.12. A fracture of the middle third of the clavicle.

humeral head and glenoid. The axial or Y-views (*Figure 4.11*) confirm that the humeral head lies posterior to the glenoid. Other forms of dislocation are very rare and often associated with severe trauma and neurovascular compromise.

Clavicular fractures

Fractures of the clavicle are frequently encountered, especially in children, and may be complicated by non-union if not immobilised. The middle third is involved in 80% of cases with the pull of sternocleidomastoid usually displacing the fragments (*Figure 4.12*). However, not all fractures are easy to detect on an AP view and a projection with 45 degree angulation may be of use if there is a high clinical suspicion. Fractures involving the distal third are less common, and may be complicated by ligamentous injury. Proximal clavicular fractures are rare.

Scapular fractures

Fractures of the scapula are uncommon and usually occur in the setting of severe blunt trauma such as a fall or a road accident. They are frequently associated with other injuries such as rib and humeral fractures as well as pulmonary trauma. The combination of scapular and clavicular fractures gives rise to a 'floating shoulder'. Most fractures will be demonstrated on the conventional AP and lateral scapular views. The majority of fractures involve the body, spine or neck of the scapula and are usually extra-articular. Extension to the glenoid may require surgical fixation. Fractures of the coracoid are usually the result of an avulsion injury from the coracoclavicular ligament or the short head of biceps. Acromial fractures typically arise from direct blunt trauma (*Figure 4.13*). Scapulothoracic dissociation is a rare and severe complication of high-impact trauma which is associated with bony, ligamentous and neurovascular damage to the upper limb.

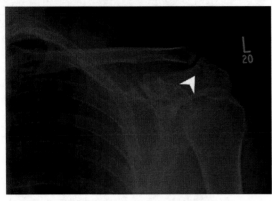

Figure 4.13. A fracture through the acromion process (arrow). The fourth rib is also fractured.

Sternoclavicular joint injury

Fracture-dislocations of the sternoclavicular joint are often the result of direct trauma. The joint may dislocate anteriorly and treatment is generally conservative. However, posterior dislocations may damage the underlying neurovascular structures and operative repair may be necessary. The appearances of these injuries may be subtle on plain radiographs and CT may be necessary to assess the extent of mediastinal injury.

Summary

Injuries to the shoulder are common and are generally straightforward to recognise on plain radiographs. It is important to make a systematic assessment of each bone and joint on at least two radiographic views. Post-reduction radiographs should always be obtained and associated fractures not overlooked.

Key points

- Shoulder injuries are frequent and may lead to disability if not recognised
- Most injuries are apparent on the AP view
- An axial or Y-view should be obtained if a dislocation is suspected
- Careful evaluation should be made of possible posterior dislocations
- Clavicular fractures are common and may be overlooked
- Acromioclavicular strains may require stress radiographs for diagnosis
- Proximal humeral fractures may be associated with wrist and hip fractures in the elderly

CHAPTER 5

Elbow and forearm

Introduction

Upper limb trauma is extremely common, with the elbow joint frequently injured. This usually occurs secondary to direct trauma or as a result of a fall onto an outstretched arm. Plain radiographs remain the first-line investigation in these patients, but interpretation can be difficult because of the variety of possible injuries, and their sometimes subtle appearances. Understanding of the anatomy, especially in the developing elbow, is key to avoiding errors in the management of these injuries. This chapter provides a systematic approach to interpreting elbow and forearm radiographs and describes the common conditions requiring these X-rays along with radiological signs.

Adult anatomy

Three joints (humero-ulnar, humeroradial and superior radio-ulnar) comprise a single synovial cavity. The distal humerus consists of the grooved trochlea and the rounded capitellum, which articulate with the ulna and radius respectively. The ulnar, radial and annular ligaments support the joint, with the latter supporting the superior radio-ulnar joint. The annular ligament attaches only to the ulna and allows the radius to rotate freely beneath it. Two depressions within the distal humerus are the coronoid (anterior) and olecranon (posterior) fossae.

Developmental anatomy

In the developing elbow, knowledge of the complex normal sequence of ossification of the epiphyseal growth plates is important (*Table 5.1*). The capitellum appears first at about 2 years of age, followed by the radial head, then the internal epicondyle. An avulsed internal epicondyle can resemble the normal trochlea, but this is easily identified as the trochlea ossifies after the internal epicondyle. The olecranon and lateral epicondyle ossify last. This can be remembered using the acronym CRITOL.

Table 5.1. Average age of appearance of secondary ossification centres

Capitellum	1 year
Radial head	3 years
Internal epicondyle	5 years
Trochlea	9–11 years
Olecranon	9–11 years
Lateral epicondyle	9–11 years

Interpretation of elbow and forearm radiographs

The routine views of the elbow include a minimum of the anteroposterior (AP) and lateral. Additional oblique views are sometimes useful for further assessment of subtle injuries, particularly of the radial head. Forearm injuries, like any other long bones, require two views taken at 90 degrees, for adequate assessment in the context of trauma.

Technical factors

- **Anteroposterior** (AP) film: The AP radiograph is taken with the patient seated, the arm abducted and fully extended, with the X-ray beam centred over the elbow joint. Sometimes the patient is not able to fully extend the arm, and so AP views of first the humerus then the forearm may be obtained.
- **Lateral** film: The lateral radiograph is taken with the arm flexed at 90 degrees, and with the forearm in supination. Optimal lateral positioning is essential for interpretation as minor degrees of obliquity or rotation can obscure fat pad abnormalities and even cause misinterpretation of fractures. However in the context of trauma patient discomfort may make this impossible.

Systematic radiological assessment

- The patient's name, date of birth and date on the film should always be checked.
- **Film quality**: As stated, optimal positioning is essential, particularly on the lateral film, as it is the most important view. The trochlea and capitellum should be superimposed, with the radius projected above the ulna. Superficial soft tissue fat and muscle planes should be visible.

- **Bony alignment:** On the lateral view, the anterior humeral line should intersect the capitellum between its middle and anterior third (*Figure 5.1a, b*). The central radial line (radiocapitellar line) should intersect the middle of the capitellum. The coronoid process of the ulna and the radial head should be superimposed. On the AP view, the radius should be continuous with the capitellum and the ulna with the trochlea (*Figure 5.2*).

- **Bony density and margins:** The cortical surfaces of all the visible bones should be systematically examined for irregularities. The internal trabecular pattern should be carefully assessed for subtle radiolucencies or bands of sclerosis, which may be the appearance of an impacted fracture. This is a particular difficulty with injuries to the radial head and neck, as approximately half of the fractures in this area are undisplaced. Like anywhere else the cortices should be smooth and regular, and depressions or steps should be considered as at least suspicious for a fracture.

- **Soft tissues**: On the lateral radiograph, the normal anterior fat pad may be visualised as a thin lucency parallel and anterior to the distal humerus. A positive fat pad sign occurs with the presence of intra-articular fluid, which includes acute blood following a fracture. The displaced fat pad is seen as a triangular lucency raised anteriorly to the humerus, and is sometimes visualised without the fracture (*Figure 5.3*). It is also occasionally absent in severe injuries as it may be obliterated because of associated haemorrhage and oedema of the capsule. A posterior fat pad is invariably only seen with a fracture (*Figure 5.4*). On the AP view, the supinator fat plane is also a useful landmark, visualised as a thin radiolucent line parallel to the cortex of the proximal radius. Soft tissue swelling may obliterate this, often when overlying an epicondyle injury.

Common errors of interpretation are shown in *Table 5.2*.

Table 5.2. Common interpretive errors

- Recognise that a visible anterior fat pad is normal, but if displaced there is a high chance of a fracture, often a subtle radial head fracture
- Absence of a fat pad does not exclude a fracture
- A radial head dislocation may just appear as an abnormal central radial line
- A supracondylar fracture may just appear as an abnormal anterior humeral line
- Fractures of the developing epicondyles can be mistaken for radiolucent epiphyseal lines
- Entrapment of the avulsed internal epicondyle epiphysis can be mistaken for the trochlear epiphysis

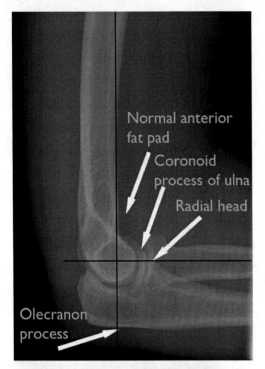

Figure 5.1. Normal lateral elbow radiograph showing the anterior humeral line (vertical line) intersecting the capitellum between its middle and anterior third. The central radial line intersects the middle of the capitellum (horizontal line). The coronoid process of the ulna and the radial head are superimposed.

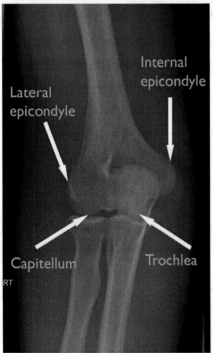

Figure 5.2. Normal AP elbow radiograph, showing the radius to be continuous with the capitellum and the ulna with the trochlea.

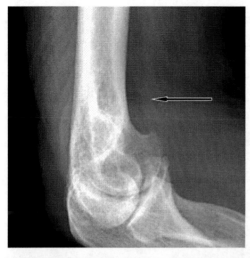

Figure 5.3. A displaced anterior fat pad is seen as a triangular lucency, raised anteriorly to the humerus (arrow). It is indicative of intra-articular fluid, which includes blood in the setting of acute trauma. As is often the case, the anterior fat pad may be visualised normally, although clinical suspicion should remain high.

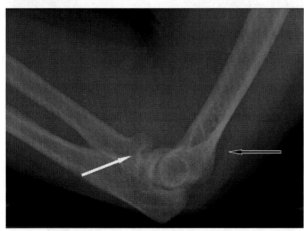

Figure 5.4. A positive posterior fat pad is invariably only seen with a fracture (black arrow). In this case, a subtle radial head fracture extending to the articular surface is visualised (white arrow).

Adult trauma

Distal humeral fractures

Injuries to the distal humerus can be intra- or extra-articular, although they are much more common in children (*Figure 5.5*). They tend to vary widely, but are commonly caused by a fall onto an outstretched arm, and it is mandatory to assess the neurovascular status of the limb. If an angular force is applied, an epicondyle fracture may occur (*Figure 5.6*). Transcondylar fractures imply a significant force, but may occur in osteoporotic bones. Fractures of the capitellum are uncommon, but can be difficult to diagnose on plain radiographs. They usually result from valgus impaction forces.

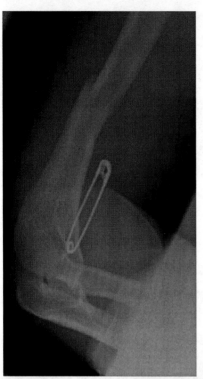

Figure 5.5. (left) A lateral elbow radiograph showing a displaced distal humeral fracture in an adult.

Figure 5.6. (below) An undisplaced lateral epicondyle fracture (black arrow) is shown with positive anterior and posterior fat pad signs (white arrows).

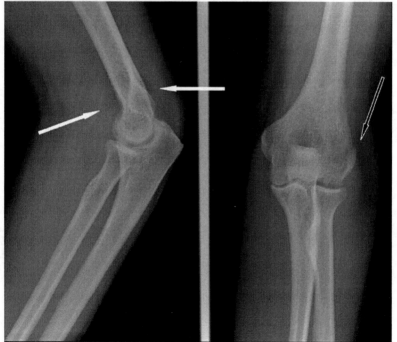

Radial head fractures

Radial head and neck fractures are the most common adult injury, accounting for over 30% of all elbow fractures. Typically caused by a fall on an outstretched hand, radial head fractures are usually orientated vertically, but radial neck fractures tend to be impacted and slightly angulated (*Figure 5.7*). Cortical breaks can be difficult to visualise, with sometimes only a slight irregularity the only clue. Positive fat pad signs are often far more evident, and should be considered significant in the appropriate clinical situation even if the radial head fracture is not visualised. Oblique views are sometimes of use in showing these fractures.

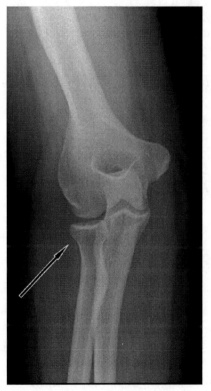

Figure 5.7. An AP elbow radiograph showing a slightly displaced linear radial head fracture (black arrow).

Elbow dislocations

Dislocations of the elbow are uncommon and usually due to valgus impaction, but almost invariably involve posterior dislocation of the radius and ulna with respect to the humerus. Fractures are frequently associated, most commonly the ulnar coronoid process, but also the internal epicondyle and radial head. They can be missed initially in the context of a potentially neurovascular threatening dislocation, but should be identified on the post-reduction radiographs, as they can act as intra-articular loose bodies and lead to incomplete reduction and late onset arthritis (*Figure 5.8*). Isolated radial head dislocations are rare in adults, and a complete examination of the ulna must be made for associated injuries. They may manifest as just an abnormal central radial line (*Figure 5.9*).

Olecranon fractures

Olecranon fractures account for approximately 20% of adult elbow injuries, and result from either a direct blow or an avulsion injury related to contraction of the triceps muscle. The transverse fracture line usually passes into the trochlear notch, but most commonly the fracture fragments are distracted due to muscular contraction (*Figure 5.10*).

Proximal forearm fractures

Usually forearm fractures involve both bones, or a single fracture and a joint disruption, although isolated injuries can occur. A midshaft ulna fracture results from a direct blow from a heavy object (termed nightstick injury, following a blow from a policeman's baton) (*Figure 5.11*). Two rare fracture-dislocation patterns are recognised in the forearm, both usually resulting from a fall onto an outstretched hand with a flexed arm. The Monteggia injury is characterised by an anteriorly angulated fracture of the proximal third of the ulna associated with an anterior dislocation of the radial head. The Galeazzi injury is characterised by a dorsally angulated distal radial fracture in conjunction with dorsal dislocation of the distal ulna. Occasionally the proximal radius and ulna may both be fractured, often in conjunction with an elbow dislocation in the context of severe trauma.

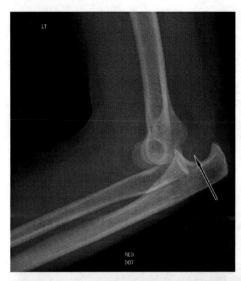

Figure 5.8. A lateral elbow radiograph showing a complete posterior elbow dislocation. Note is also made of a subtle avulsed bony fragment which is lying within the joint (black arrow), which can lead to incomplete reduction and late onset arthritis.

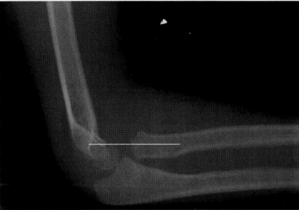

Figure 5.9. A lateral elbow radiograph showing an isolated radial head dislocation. The central radial line (radiocapitellar line) (white line) is displaced and is the only sign of this subtle injury.

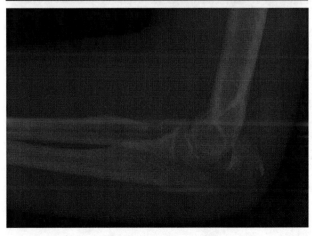

Figure 5.10. A lateral elbow radiograph showing an olecranon fracture. The fracture fragments are distracted due to muscular contraction. Note the absence of displaced fat pads, due to capsular rupture.

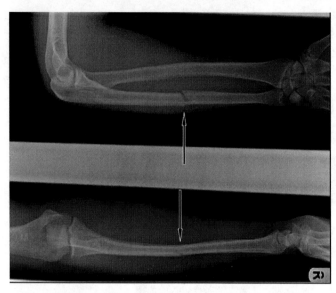

Figure 5.1 1.
Forearm
radiographs
showing an
isolated midshaft
ulna fracture. This
resulted from a
direct blow from
a heavy object
(black arrows).

Child trauma

Many of the injuries described above may also occur in children, but specific paediatric trauma will now be discussed.

Supracondylar fracture

Supracondylar fractures are the commonest elbow fracture in children, making up 60% of all elbow fractures in this age group, and are usually caused by a fall onto an outstretched hand. Usually a transverse fracture passes just proximal to the capitellum and trochlea, with the distal fragment often posteriorly displaced. The anterior humeral line passes through the anterior third of the capitellum or even completely anterior to it (*Figure 5.12*). Severely displaced fractures may cause neurovascular compromise, and early reduction is key (*Figure 5.13*). Undisplaced fractures are often missed, but a positive posterior fad pad sign is almost always present.

Epicondylar injuries

Epicondyle injuries are the second most common elbow fracture in childhood, with the lateral epicondylar fracture making up 15% of elbow fractures. They can be extensive, involving also the capitellum, trochlea and distal humeral metaphysis (*Figure 5.12*). This is not always appreciated if only the capitellum is ossified. Internal epicondylar epiphyseal avulsions occur in relation to elbow dislocations, and also in isolation due to valgus stress (*Figure 5.14*). The avulsed epiphysis is usually displaced inferiorly, but it may pass intra-articularly. In this situation it may be misinterpreted as being one of the other ossification centres. Remembering the normal sequence of ossification will assist diagnosis (*Table 5.1*), as if the trochlear epiphysis is present, the internal epicondyle epiphysis must also be present, and may be avulsed and not immediately obvious. Positive fat pad signs may help, and in difficult cases a radiograph of the uninjured side may be of use.

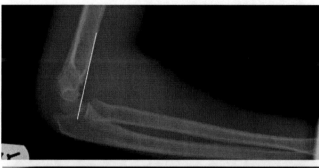

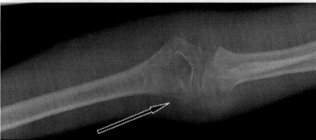

Figure 5.12. AP and lateral radiographs show a transverse fracture of the distal humerus that passes just proximally to the capitellum and trochlea, and into the lateral epicondyle, with the distal fragment posteriorly displaced (black arrow). The anterior humeral line passes through the anterior cortex of the capitellum (line).

Figure 5.13. A lateral elbow radiograph showing a severely displaced supracondylar fracture, with the anterior humeral line passing completely anteriorly to the capitellum. With severely displaced injuries such as this, neurovascular compromise may occur.

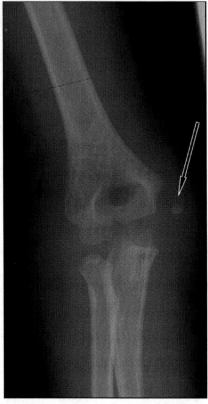

Figure 5.14. An AP elbow radiograph showing an internal epicondylar epiphyseal avulsion. The avulsed epiphysis is displaced inferiorly (black arrow), and occurred due to sudden valgus stress.

Pulled elbow

Pulled elbow occurs in children between 1 and 4 years of age, and occurs when there is a sudden pull on the pronated extended arm, such as when the child is suddenly lifted by the hand. It occurs due to momentary distraction of the radiocapitellar joint, allowing subluxation of the radial head out of the angular ligament. Radiographs are usually normal.

Further imaging

Further imaging of elbow injuries is rarely required, but occasionally, computed tomography is performed to assist the surgeon pre-operatively where the fracture is complicated and/or not adequately delineated on plain films (*Figure 5.15*).

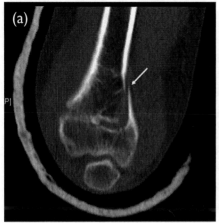 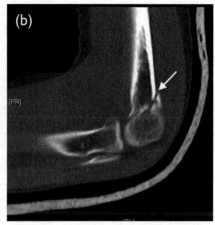

Figure 5.15. (a) Coronal and (b) sagittal computed tomography images of the left elbow in a plaster of Paris. This shows a supracondylar fracture (arrows) of the distal humerus extending into the epiphyseal plate and into the joint space. This study has been performed to allow the orthopaedic surgeon to plan surgery appropriately as the original plain film images (not shown) had not adequately delineated the fracture.

Key points

- Always check the patient's name and age and date of film
- Assess film quality
- Assess alignment, particularly anterior humeral and radio-capitellar lines on the lateral radiograph
- Assess bony cortices for subtle fractures
- Assess soft tissues for positive fat pad signs. The presence of a posterior fat pad is always abnormal. A visible anterior fat pad is normal
- CRITOL is the most common sequence for the appearance of the secondary ossification centres in children

Chapter 6

Wrist and hand

Introduction

Wrist and hand injuries account for approximately 15% of casualty department attendances. Recognition of injuries in this area is important as apparently minor injuries can result in significant loss of function. Early detection and appropriate management usually results in full recovery of normal function.

Adult anatomy

The adult wrist consists of eight carpal bones arranged in proximal (scaphoid, lunate, triquetrum and pisiform) and distal (trapezium, trapezoid, capitate and hamate) rows. These form three articulations: the radiocarpal, carpocarpal and carpometacarpal joints. The distal radius articulates with the lunate and scaphoid and is supported by strong radiocarpal and intercarpal ligaments. The distal radio-ulnar joint includes the triangular fibrocartilage that allows pronation and supination at the wrist. The carpocarpal and carpometacarpal joints are supported by strong ligaments. As in the foot the first three metacarpals articulate with their own carpal bone: trapezium, trapezoid and capitate while the fourth and fifth metacarpals share the hamate.

The metacarpal and phalanges articulate via synovial joints. There are strong radial and ulna collateral ligaments that prevent sideways movements at the metacarpophalangeal (MCP) and proximal interphalangeal (PIP) joints. The capsule of the interphalangeal and metacarpophalangeal joints is thickened on the volar (palmar) aspect and forms a dense fibrous structure called the volar plate that attaches to the adjacent phalanx. Each finger has two flexor tendons and one extensor tendon that inserts into the base of the phalanges.

Developmental anatomy

The carpal bones begin to ossify from 1–2 years onwards and are all present by 5–6 years. The scaphoid and trapezoid are the last ones to ossify. The primary ossification centres for the metacarpals and phalanges are already present at birth. Secondary ossification centres (epiphyses) appear for the base of the first metacarpal, heads of the other metacarpals and bases of the phalanges at about 2–3 years. Fusion of the growth plates occurs at 17 years. Biological skeletal age can be ascertained from left hand and wrist films up until puberty.

Interpretation of wrist and hand radiographs

Technical factors

Wrist

- **Anteroposterior (AP) view**: This should include the distal radius and ulna as well as radiocarpal joint, carpometacarpal joints and metacarpal bases.
- **Lateral view**: This is mainly used to assess radiocarpal alignment and to identify carpal dislocations.
  Scaphoid views: These will be discussed in more detail below.

Hand

- The optimal radiographic projection will depend upon detailed clinical information.
- **Anteroposterior (AP) and oblique** views of the entire hand are indicated for injuries to the metacarpals or phalanges.
- **Anteroposterior (AP) and lateral** views of individual digit or thumb injuries are recommended.

Systematic radiological assessment

- The patient's name, date of birth and date on the film should always be checked.
- **Film quality:** On wrist films the radius and ulna should be superimposed to avoid spurious diagnosis of dislocation of the distal ulna. Similarly on the Posteroanterior (PA) wrist view there should be no overlap of the distal radius and ulna due to rotation.
- **Bone and joint alignment:** The metacarpal bases, radius, lunate and capitate articulate with each other lying in a straight line on the lateral view of the wrist. The joint spaces should be parallel and uniform in width (1–2mm). On the PA wrist three parallel arcs may be drawn joining the articular margins of the carpal bones. The first arc consists of proximal articular margins of the scaphoid, lunate and

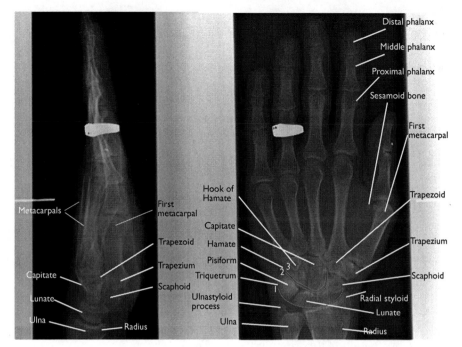

Figure 6.1. Normal AP and lateral radiographs of the wrist and hand with annotations.

triquetrum, the second by joining the distal articular margins of the proximal carpal row and the third by joining the proximal articular margins of the capitate and hamate (*Figure 6.1*). Disruption of these parallel lines indicates subluxation or dislocation of the carpal bones. On hand films the phalanges and metacarpals of each finger and thumb should be normally aligned on both views (*Figure 6.1*).

• **Bone margins**: The cortical margins of all the bones should be inspected on two views to exclude a fracture. Also check bone density and trabecular pattern. Sclerotic bands may be the only sign of an impacted fracture. Vascular channels need to be distinguished from fractures. Vascular channels are often seen in the distal shaft of the phalanges and appear as thin, radiolucent lines that run obliquely from the external proximal surface entering the medullary canal distally.

There are numerous accessory ossicles or sesamoid bones around the wrist and hand. These occupy classic positions and have well-corticated margins as opposed to the irregular edges of fracture fragments.

• **Soft tissues**: Use a bright light to look for soft tissue swelling as this may be the only indicator of injury. Note foreign bodies.

Rigorous radiological assessment may help to avoid common interpretative errors encountered in casualty (*Table 6.1*).

Wrist injuries

Most wrist injuries are caused by a fall on the outstretched hand in which the force is transmitted across the scaphoid waist and carpocarpal joint.

Distal radial fractures

Colles' fracture

This is a fracture of the distal radius with dorsal displacement of the distal fragment producing a 'dinner fork deformity' on the lateral view (*Figure 6.2*). It may be associated with a fracture of the ulnar styloid process and scaphoid.

Table 6.1. Common interpretive errors

- Wrong patient/date. Side marker on film erroneously applied
- Mistaking sesamoid bones/accessory ossicles for fractures. Sesamoid bones/accessory ossicles have well-corticated, smooth, rounded margins. Consult a book if unsure, e.g. Atlas of Normal Roentgen Variants That May Simulate Disease (Keats and Anderson, 2006)
- Mistaking soft tissue creases as fractures. If a line extends beyond the cortical margin it is not a fracture. Also do not confuse a vascular groove for a fracture
- Poor radiography may mask injuries:
  - Dislocations, avulsion fractures of the volar plate, and fractures extending to the articular surfaces may be missed on poorly positioned lateral views
  - Avulsion fractures affecting the collateral ligaments may be missed on poorly positioned posterio-anterior views.
  Therefore, repeat the film if it is of poor quality
- Closure of the distal radial epiphysis may leave a dense line that should not be diagnosed as an impacted fracture

Smith's fracture

This is also known as a 'reverse Colles' fracture' in which there is anterior displacement of the distal fracture fragment.

Barton's fracture

This is a fracture of the dorsal aspect of the radius that extends to the wrist joint. A 'reverse Barton's fracture' occurs on the volar aspect and also extends to the articular surface. Fractures that involve the articular surface carry a poorer prognosis due to the increased incidence of articular cartilage damage and therefore premature osteoarthritis.

Chauffeur's fracture

This is a fracture of the radial styloid process.

Galeazzi fracture

This is a distal radial fracture associated with a dorsal dislocation of the distal radioulnar joint that has already been covered in *Chapter 5*.

Carpal fractures

The scaphoid is the most commonly fractured carpal bone (90%). Clinically a fracture is suggested by anatomical snuffbox tenderness. A scaphoid film series consists of a PA, lateral and two oblique views. If no fracture is seen but is still strongly suspected clinically a follow up film 10–14 days later is mandatory by which time the fracture may be seen as a lucent or dense line. In fact patients in whom a scaphoid series has been performed should have follow up films whether or not a fracture has been demonstrated. Scaphoid fractures may also be demonstrated by MR, bone scan or CT. Eighty percent of scaphoid fractures are across the waist. Since the blood supply to the proximal pole enters via the distal pole there is a risk of non-union and avascular necrosis if the patient is incorrectly managed (*Figure 6.3*).

Triquetral fractures are the second commonest carpal bone fracture. It is recognised as a fragment of bone seen posterior to the carpal bones on the lateral view (*Figure 6.4*).

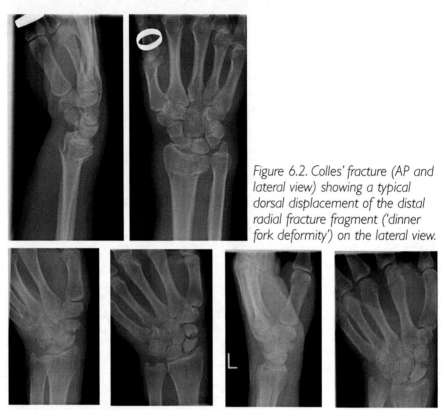

Figure 6.2. Colles' fracture (AP and lateral view) showing a typical dorsal displacement of the distal radial fracture fragment ('dinner fork deformity') on the lateral view.

Figure 6.3. Scaphoid series with non-union of a scaphoid waist fracture complicated by avascular necrosis of the proximal pole (seen as a sclerotic fragment).

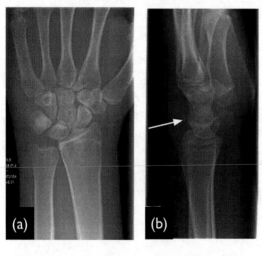

Figure 6.4. Triquetral fracture best seen on the (a) lateral view as a bony fragment dorsal to the carpal bones (arrow). On the (b) AP view the fracture cannot be visualised. This case illustrates the importance of imaging trauma cases in two planes to avoid missing bony injuries. Reproduced with permission from Harvey et al. (2005) Self-Assessment Cases in Surgical Imaging. Oxford University Press.

Carpal dislocations

Lunate dislocation

In this type the lunate bone dislocates anteriorly. It is best diagnosed on the lateral view and is recognised by the abnormal anterior site of the lunate while the radius articulates erroneously with the capitate (*Figure 6.5*). On the PA view the lunate has a triangular shape rather than its normal quadrilateral shape and there is loss of joint space between the scaphoid and lunate.

Perilunate dislocation

In this type the lunate remains correctly sited and the rest of the carpus is dislocated dorsally (*Figure 6.6*). Again it is best diagnosed on the lateral view and is often associated with a scaphoid fracture (trans scapho-perilunate dislocation).

Carpal subluxations

Ligamentous rupture will result in widening (>2mm) of the intercarpal joints. A well-recognised example is the scapholunate ligament rupture (rotatory dislocation of the scaphoid) seen on the PA view as widening of the scapholunate joint (Madonna or Terry Thomas sign) (*Figure 6.7*).

Child trauma

The wrist is a common site of trauma in children and dealt with more fully in *Chapter 14*. Epiphyseal, metaphyseal and greenstick injuries should be looked for. A greenstick fracture is seen as a break in one cortex with bending of the other, associated with angulation (*Figure 6.8*). A torus fracture is seen as bucking of both cortices without angulation (*Figure 6.8*).

The Salter-Harris classification of epiphyseal injuries should be known and applied (see *Chapter 14*).

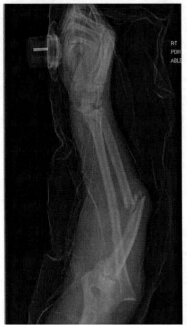

Figure 6.5. Lunate dislocation with Monteggio fracture (fracture of the ulnar with dislocation of the radial head).

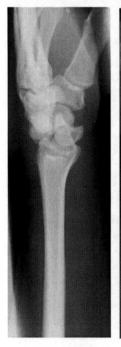 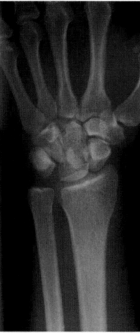

Figure 6.6. Perilunate dislocation. On the lateral view there is dorsal dislocation of the distal carpal row. The lunate bone articulates normally with the radius although there is some rotation, giving it a triangular appearance on the AP film. Also there is loss of the normal joint space between the proximal and distal carpal rows on the AP view indicative of dislocation. Reproduced with permission from Harvey et al. (2005) Self-Assessment Cases in Surgical Imaging. Oxford University Press.

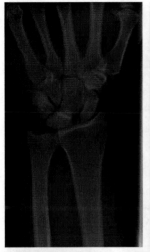
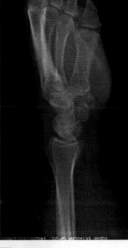

Figure 6.7. There is widening of the scapholunate joint space (arrow) indicative of rupture of the scapholunate ligament (Madonna or Terry Thomas sign).

Figure 6.8. AP and lateral views of the forearm showing a greenstick fracture of the radius with angulation (chevron) and a torus fracture of the ulna (arrow).

Hand injuries

Thumb injuries

Bennett's fracture

Bennett's fracture is a fracture of the base of the first metacarpal extending into the carpometacarpal joint with dislocation at the latter (*Figure 6.9*). The metacarpal is pulled dorsally and medially by the abductor pollicis longus muscle which inserts into its base. Since it is an unstable fracture, referral to a hand surgeon is suggested as it may require open reduction and internal fixation.

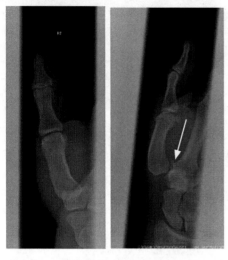

Figure 6.9. Bennett's fracture. There is a fracture of the base of the 1st metacarpal (arrow) with dislocation of the metacarpal due to pull of the abductor pollicis longus muscle.

Gamekeeper's or skier's thumb

Gamekeeper's or skier's thumb is due to a rupture or sprain of the ulnar collateral ligament at the first metacarpophalangeal joint secondary to forceful abduction of the thumb. Occasionally it may be associated with an avulsion fracture. Radiographs may be normal or only show soft tissue swelling. A stress view may demonstrate instability of the joint. A complete tear of the ligament requires surgical repair.

Metacarpal and phalangeal fractures

Most fractures involve the mid shaft of the metacarpal or phalanx; they are stable and only require strapping (*Figure 6.10*).

Certain fractures require referral to a hand surgeon:

- Avulsion fractures of a bone fragment from the base of a phalanx.
- Spiral fractures of the shaft with rotation of the fragments, as internal fixation may be required.
- Extension of the fracture to a joint surface.

Boxer's fracture

Boxer's fracture is a fracture of the neck of the fifth metacarpal and is usually associated with volar angulation of the head (*Figure 6.11*).

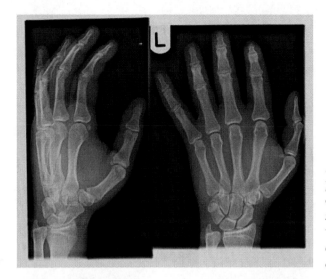

Figure 6.10. Oblique fractures of the 3rd and 4th metacarpal shafts. Note that there is no extension of the fracture to the articular surface.

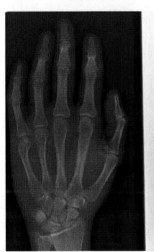 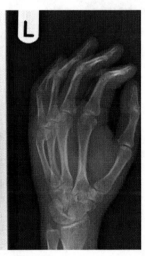

Figure 6.11. Subtle fracture of the neck of the 5th metacarpal with some volar augulation (arrow), best seen on the oblique view.

Avulsion fractures

Avulsion fractures are fragments of bone avulsed at the insertion of collateral ligaments (medial or lateral avulsion), volar plate (palmar avulsion) (*Figure 6.12*) or extensor tendons (dorsal avulsion).

These injuries may appear trivial but can cause significant hand dysfunction if missed.

Mallet injury

This is caused by rupture or avulsion of the extensor tendon from the terminal phalanx. A bone fragment is only present in approximately 25% of cases. Clinical examination reveals a flexion deformity of the terminal phalanx that cannot be extended. Management of a closed mallet injury is by splintage in a mallet splint.

Interphalangeal dislocations

Dislocation most commonly affects the proximal interphalangeal joint. Dislocation is best demonstrated on the lateral view (*Figure 6.13*). Radiographs should be repeated after reduction to look for fractures and check for satisfactory joint alignment. Incongruity may indicate the presence of soft tissue in the joint, e.g. torn volar plate.

Carpo-metacarpal dislocations

The fourth and fifth joints are most commonly affected and may be associated with a fracture of the base of the metacarpal.

Finger tip injuries

These injuries are most commonly due to a crush fracture (*Figure 6.14*). Fractures may involve the nail bed or joint space.

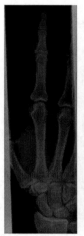
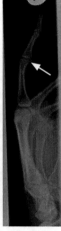
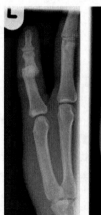
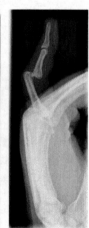

Figure 6.12. (left) Avulsion fracture of the base of the middle phalanx of the index finger at the insertion of the volar plate (arrow).

Figure 6.13. (right) Volar dislocation at the proximal interphalangeal joint of the 5th finger.

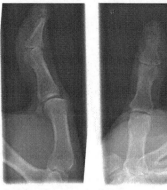

Figure 6.14. Compound crush fracture of the terminal phalanx complicated by osteomyelitis seen as bony destruction superimposed on a fracture.

Soft tissue injuries

Radiographs may be used to identify radio-opaque foreign (glass and metal) bodies but ultrasound is better for radiolucent objects (wood and plastic). When trying to detect a foreign body a metallic marker should be placed at the site of the injury, tangential to the site of injury. See *Chapter 13* for further discussion.

Key points

- Always check the patient's name and age and date of the film
- Assess film quality
- Recognition of injuries in the wrist and hand is important as apparently minor injuries can result in significant dysfunction. Early detection and appropriate management usually results in full recovery of normal function. Therefore the principle of imaging an injury in two planes is particularly important in the wrist and hand
- Exclude a fracture by examining the cortical contour of every bone on two views. Use a bright light for this. Do not confuse a vascular groove for a fracture
- If a scaphoid fracture is suspected, perform a scaphoid series. Follow up is mandatory whether or not a fracture has been demonstrated
- Inspect the lateral view of the wrist for a carpal dislocation or a fracture of the posterior radial cortex
- Look carefully for subtle greenstick and torus fractures in children
- Referral to a hand specialist is indicated in:
  - Fractures that extend to an articular surface
  - Bony avulsions
  - Spiral fractures with rotation
  - Unstable fractures, e.g. Bennett's injury

- With dislocations look for an associated fracture, e.g. scaphoid fracture in a perilunate dislocation

References

Keats TE, Anderson MW eds. (2006) *Atlas of Normal Roentgen Variants That May Simulate Disease* (8th Edn). St Louis, Mosby

CHAPTER 7

Skull and facial bones

Introduction

There are few indications for the skull X-ray as it has been superseded by head computed tomography (CT) as the initial investigation in head trauma (National Institute for Health and Clinical Excellence, 2007). However, facial radiographs remain the first-line investigation for facial trauma, and also for a number of other conditions that may present in the accident and emergency department. This chapter provides a systematic approach to interpreting skull and facial films and describes the common conditions requiring these X-rays along with radiological signs.

Interpretation of the skull radiograph

Technical factors

- **Radiographic projections**: The views required will depend on the indication. In a head injury a lateral view supplemented by either an occipitofrontal or Towne's view is performed.
- **Lateral** film: The patient lies on the X-ray couch with the side of the head on the film cassette. This is the most commonly required view (*Figure 7.1*), and is performed by a technique known as horizontal beam radiography. This means that the X-ray beam is in the same horizontal plane as the supine patient, such that an air-fluid level can be demonstrated in the sphenoid sinus.
- **Posteroanterior (PA) (occipitofrontal)** film: The patient lies prone on the X-ray couch with forehead on the film cassette.
- **Towne's (AP)** film: The patient lies supine on the X-ray couch with occiput on the film cassette (*Figure 7.2*). This view is contraindicated in suspected cervical injury.

Systematic radiological assessment

- The patient's name, date of birth and date on the film should always be checked.

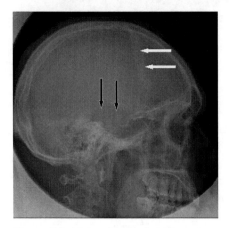

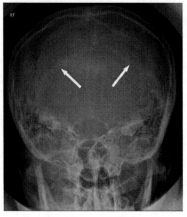

Figure 7.1. Normal lateral skull radiograph. Note normal vascular markings (black arrows) and coronal skull suture (white arrows).

Figure 7.2. Normal Towne's view of skull. Normal lambdoid skull sutures are marked (white arrows).

- **Film quality**: The film projection should be checked (i.e. PA, AP, lateral). The first cervical vertebra should be visible on the lateral film. The exposure, film centring and rotation should be checked for adequacy. On the lateral view the anterior clinoid processes and posterior margins of the mandibles should be superimposed. Glasses and earrings should be removed.

- **Linear markings**: Skull vascular markings are caused by blood vessels marking an impression on the bones of the vault, resulting in branching linear lucencies. These can be difficult to distinguish from vault fractures, but are often more faint as they only involve the inner table of the skull, and also may have a sclerotic margin (*Table 7.1*). Normal anatomical skull sutures should also be distinguished from skull fractures. They exhibit symmetrical anatomical position and have fine sclerotic or corticated margins. Sutures are not as translucent as fractures. Fractures may occur along a suture causing diastasis. In children raised intracranial pressure may result in widening of sutures a few days after a head injury but this rarely occurs in adults. Small irregular lucencies can sometimes be seen near the vertex, caused by normal arachnoid granulations.

  Skull vault thickness is non-uniform, often very thick frontally and at the occipital protruberances. It may be normally thinned in the parietal regions.

- **Aerated structures:** The paranasal sinuses should be inspected (see facial radiograph section below). Aerated mastoid air cells should be present bilaterally.

Table 7.1. Distinguishing fractures from vascular markings

Vascular marking	Fracture
Sclerotic margin	Absent sclerotic margin
Grey/black density (only inner table of skull involved)	Black density (both inner and outer tables of skull bone involved)
Occur in anatomical sites	Occur in non-anatomical sites
Branches taper peripherally	Branch abruptly

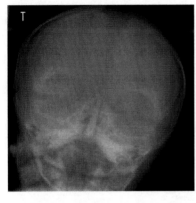

Figure 7.3. Skull radiograph in the neonate. Note is made of opacification of the paranasal sinuses. This is a normal appearance at birth, as the paranasal sinuses aerate over the first few years of life.

- **Calcifications**: A number of normal calcifications can be present intracranially, including the pineal gland (50% over 20 years), basal ganglia and choroid plexus. The dura may calcify anywhere, but most commonly this is seen in the falx and tentorium cerebelli. Arachnoid granulations can also calcify as can any intracerebral artery, but most commonly this occurs in the internal cerebral artery in the region of the siphon. The lens of the eye may calcify. Abnormal calcification is seen in tumours (meningioma, craniopharyngioma, glioma), aneurysms and arteriovenous malformations (AVMs).
- **The skull base**: The pituitary fossa should be visualised on the lateral film, and may occasionally be 'J-shaped', which is a normal variant.
- **The developing skull**: At birth the cranial bones may overlap due to in-utero moulding, but this normally resolves within a week. Also at birth, the sinuses are not aerated, developing with the facial skeleton over the first few years of life (*Figure 7.3*). Small lateral fontanelles normally close by 3 months, the posterior fontanelle normally closes by 8 months, and the anterior fontanelle by 18 months. Accessory sutures are more common in children, and can be unilateral, often mistaken for fractures. The frontal bone is divided in two by the

Table 7.2. Common interpretive errors

- Mistaking normal vascular markings or normal skull sutures for linear fractures
- Missing a depressed skull fracture, seen as a double density or as a dense white line
- Missing an air fluid level in the sphenoid sinus, indicative of a base of skull fracture
- Missing a 'blow out' fracture. Subtle soft tissue in the roof of the maxillary antrum
- Missing a second, more subtle mandibular fracture

metopic suture, which usually fuses by 2 years but may persist into adulthood. The mendosal suture (accessory occipital suture) may also persist into adulthood. The major sutures narrow with the suture width decreasing from 1cm at birth to 2mm by 3 years old.
- **Indications**: There are few indications for skull radiographs, now that head CT is the first line investigation for head trauma.
Common errors of interpretation are shown in *Table 7.2*.

Traumatic indications

In moderate and more severe head injuries, patients should be referred directly for a head CT, as stated in guidelines from the National Institute for Health and Clinical Excellence (2007). Patients who have lost consciousness, have significant amnesia, cerebrospinal fluid leak from ear or nose, suspected penetrating injury or foreign body, suffered an epileptic fit, repeated episodes of vomiting or any neurological deficit should be considered in this category. In more mild injuries, in an alert and orientated patient, there is still a role for the skull radiograph, although usually only to assess for soft tissue foreign bodies. However, occasionally on such a study, a skull fracture may be revealed (*Figure 7.4*). A depressed skull fracture can be more difficult to diagnose, as it may appear only as a dense white line or double density due to overlapping bone fragments. A fluid level in the sphenoid sinus is only detected on a lateral film, and is a strong indicator that a base of skull fracture has occurred (*Figure 7.5*). The presence of intracranial air is a rare but important sign, as this implies a fracture has occurred through a sinus (*Figure 7.5*). This is typically seen as an abnormal lucency within the lateral ventricles or at the base of the brain, and often results from penetrating trauma (*Figure 7.6a–c*). If a skull fracture is diagnosed, the head injury should be re-classified as moderate to severe. Although a fracture is an important sign of a head injury, it bears little correlation to underlying brain damage, and the patient should be referred for an urgent head CT to assess for any possible intracranial injuries (*Figure 7.7a, b*).

Assessment of the craniocervical junction and atlanto-axial joint (abnormal if more than 3mm in adults and 5mm in children) should also be performed routinely. In cases of severe head injury a whole cervical spine CT should be performed as routine in accompaniment to a head CT, as the incidence of associated injury in this region is very high, and the patient almost impossible to assess. Other further imaging of the head and face is rarely required. Cranial magnetic resonance imaging (MRI), in particular, is rarely indicated in the trauma setting.

Non-traumatic indications

In the emergency setting, the indications are again few, but a skull radiograph will detect skull bony abnormalities. Patients who have had previous neurosurgery for hydrocephalus and have a ventriculoperitoneal shunt, may occasionally require a skull radiograph to assess the position of the shunt (*Figure 7.8*).

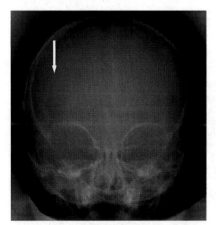

Figure 7.4. A frontal radiograph showing a linear skull fracture through the right parietal bone (arrow).

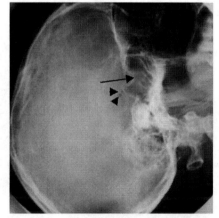

Figure 7.5. A lateral horizontal beam skull radiograph showing an air fluid level in the sphenoid sinus (arrow), and intracranial air (arrowheads). In the context of head trauma, these are indicators that a base of skull fracture has occurred. Reproduced with permission from Harvey et al. (2005) Self-Assessment Cases in Surgical Imaging. Oxford University Press.

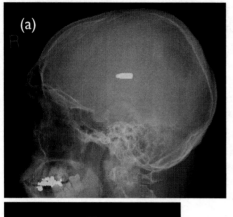

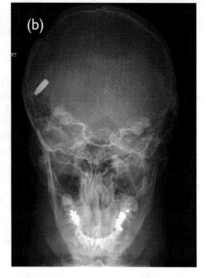

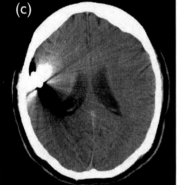

Figures 7.6. Plain skull radiographs (a, b) (above) and an axial CT image (c) (left) showing an AK-47 rifle bullet intracranially, embedded within the right side of the brain. There is also a post-surgical rounded bony defect within the right parietal bone.

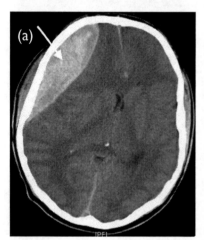

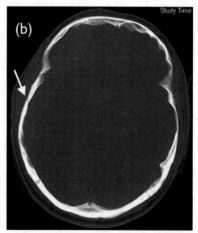

Figure 7.7. Axial CT images showing a large extradural haematoma (a) abutting the right frontal lobe and causing significant mass effect on the underlying brain (arrow). (b) Bony windows on the same study show an underlying skull fracture (arrow).

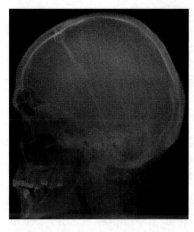

Figure 7.8. Lateral skull radiograph, showing a ventriculoperitoneal shunt in a patient with treated hydrocephalus.

Interpretation of facial radiographs

Technical factors

- **Radiographic projections:** For most indications three standard views are normally adequate. These consist of two tilted frontal views, with differing degrees of angulation, termed the occipitomental (OM) view and OM30 view, and also a lateral view (the least useful). Occasionally, a submentovertical (SMV) view is required, in which the ethmoid and sphenoid sinuses are visualised, and also the skull base. An orthopantomogram (OPG) is a specialised view of the mandible which utilises a technique called tomography, where the X-ray tube and film move in opposite directions, and generate a panoramic image of the jaw, while blurring out other structures. Additional views will be discussed in the appropriate clinical contexts.

Systematic radiological assessment

- The patient's name, date of birth and date on the film should always be checked.
- **Film quality:** The film projection should be checked (i.e. OM, OM30, lateral). The mandible should be visible on the frontal films. Glasses and earrings should be removed.

Interpretation

A useful system for inspecting the frontal facial views utilises a series of lines traced over the radiograph, termed McGrigor's lines (*Figure 7.9*).

Soft tissue swelling, sutural widening, air-fluid levels and any fractures should be observed, with particular attention to symmetry between the injured and uninjured sides. Line 1 passes through the frontozygomatic suture at the lateral margin of the orbit, and then runs over the superior orbital margin and across into the frontal sinus, before passing across the same structures, in reverse, on the contralateral side. Line 2 passes along the superior border of the zygomatic arch (likened to an elephant's trunk), crosses the zygomatic body, and onto the inferior orbital margin, before passing up to the bridge of the nose and to the contralateral side. Line 3 passes along the inferior border of the zygomatic arch (the elephant's trunk), along the lateral border of the maxilla, around the lateral and inferior margins of the maxillary antrum, and across to the contralateral side. Lines 4 and 5 relate to the superior and inferior surfaces of the mandible.

- **Paranasal sinuses**: The maxillary sinuses and ethmoidal air cells should be fully aerated. The frontal and sphenoid sinuses may have widely varying pneumatisation, and are often asymmetrical. The maxillary sinuses appear radiographically a few weeks after birth, while the others appear over the first few years of life. A fluid level in the sphenoid sinus in the context of trauma implies a skull base fracture has occurred.
- **Bony anatomy**: The orbits, zygomatic arches, nasal bone and mandible should all be inspected. The zygomatic sutures should not be widened. On the frontal views, in the context of trauma, the uninjured side is a useful 'normal' comparison.

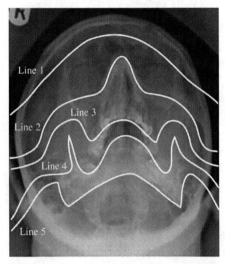

Figure 7.9. A normal angled occipitomental view of the face, overlaid with McGrigor's lines, used to identify bony or soft tissue injuries.

Traumatic indications

Facial skeleton

Facial fractures are common. Patients presenting with facial injuries should have an early airway assessment, prior to radiological investigation, as this can be compromised, particularly in severe mandibular injuries. Plain radiography remains the first-line investigation, with cross-sectional imaging reserved for more specialised indications. Cortical breach is the most important sign of a fracture, although secondary signs include soft tissue swelling, sinus opacification or air-fluid level, and abnormal air. Abnormal air includes subcutaneous emphysema, intraorbital and intracranial air, all of which are highly suggestive of a fracture of an aerated sinus.

Orbital fractures

A direct blow to the front of the orbit may produce an orbital 'blow-out' fracture. The blow transmits force to the orbital rim, which in turn transmits the force to its weaker medial wall or, more commonly, floor, where the fracture occurs. If the floor fractures, normally only fat passes through into the maxillary sinus, although sometimes the inferior and even the medial rectus muscle may herniate through the fracture defect. Failure to recognise this may result in permanent symptomatology. Diplopia may be the only clinical sign of this, and that itself may be secondary to periorbital haemorrhage or a number of other post-traumatic disturbances. Radiologically the only sign may be a soft tissue opacity in the upper part of the maxillary sinus (the 'teardrop' sign), as often the fractures are completely undisplaced and not visualised (*Figure 7.10*). Intra-orbital air is a useful sign when present (*Figure 7.11*), although antral opacification or air-fluid level are not specific. Fracture of the medial wall is usually not particularly clinically significant.

Nasal fractures

These are extremely common and often isolated injuries. They should be assessed clinically and do not require imaging, except in medicolegal contexts, when a lateral film is usually sufficient.

Frontal fractures

These are uncommon, and usually accompany other injuries in the context of more severe trauma. There is an association with underlying brain injury, and a CT is more appropriate in this setting.

Ethmoidal fractures

An isolated naso-ethmoidal injury is uncommon, typically produced by a high energy blow to the upper nose by a small object. Associated eye and intracranial injuries are common.

Zygomatic arch fractures

The zygomatic arch can be seen on the OM, Towne's, OF and SMV views. The 'tripod' fracture is a common injury in which the zygoma can detach from the remainder of the facial skeleton. The arch of the zygoma and body of the zygoma both fracture, and the fronto-zygomatic suture widens (*Figure 7.12*).

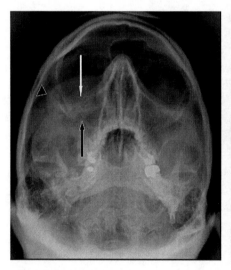

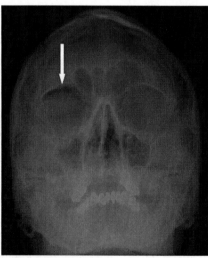

Figure 7.10. An orbital 'blow-out' fracture. Soft tissue is seen superiorly within the right maxillary antrum consistent with herniated orbital contents (black arrow). There is a fracture of the inferior right orbital margin (white arrow), with associated periorbital soft tissue swelling (arrowhead).

Figure 7.11. Occipitofrontal view of the skull, showing orbital emphysema (arrow).

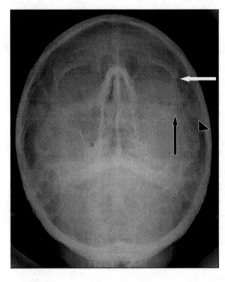

Figure 7.12. A 'tripod' fracture. A large amount of soft tissue swelling overlies the bony injuries. A widened left fronto-zygomatic suture (white arrow), a fracture through the body of the zygoma (black arrow) and a fracture through the zygomatic arch (arrowhead) are shown.

Complex facial fractures

These have been classified according to the Le Fort system, which defines three patterns of fracture following severe blunt facial trauma (*Table 7.3*). In a Le Fort I fracture the lower maxilla becomes separated from the rest of the face. In a Le Fort II fracture a central pyramidal fracture occurs. Complete craniofacial separation occurs in a Le Fort III fracture (*Figure 7.13*). In practice many facial injuries do not fit into a pattern of Le Fort fractures but the classification is still employed for descriptive purposes.

Table 7.3. The Le Fort fracture classification

Le Fort I	Separation of the upper jaw. The alveolar surface of the maxilla separates from the main part of the maxilla, with fractures through the medial wall and floor of each maxillary sinus, and through the lower nasal septum in the midline
Le Fort II	A central pyramid shaped fragment is separated. Fractures occur through the nasal septum, the maxillary sinuses and the inferior and medial walls of the orbits
Le Fort III	Separation of the entire facial skeleton from the skull base. Fractures occur through the nasal septum, medial and lateral walls of the orbits and through the zygomatic arches

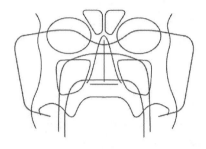

Figure 7.13. A schematic diagram showing the fracture lines in Le Fort I, II and III fractures (see text for description).

Mandibular fractures

Normally oblique views supplementing a frontal film are adequate. Other views such as an OPG may be required, for example to demonstrate dental injuries. The mandible should be considered as a bony ring. It will usually fracture in two places. Classically an obvious fracture will occur at the site of impact (symphysis) (*Figure 7.14*), and a subtle fracture where the force dissipates (condylar neck) (*Figure 7.15*), although the ramus, body and angle also commonly fracture. If a fracture involves a tooth bearing surface, it should be considered an open fracture. Injury to the temporomandibular joint is rare, and best demonstrated on CT. Severe mandibular injuries may cause airway compromise.

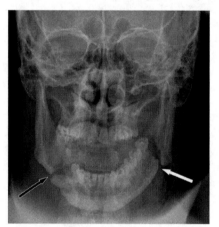

Figure 7.14. A fracture of the right body (black arrow) and left angle of the mandible (white arrow). The mandible should be considered as a bony ring as it will usually fracture in two places.

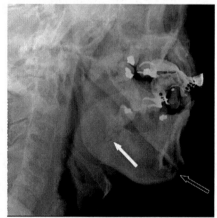

Figure 7.15. A left-sided oblique view of the mandible showing a fracture of the symphysis menti (black arrow). An additional fracture is seen extending through the angle of the mandible (white arrow), which was not visualised on the frontal view (not shown).

Non-traumatic indications

In the accident and emergency setting, there are few non-traumatic indications for facial radiographs. For orbital foreign bodies, frontal views can be performed in both upward and downward gaze, in order to localise the foreign body, although further investigation with CT or ultrasound is increasingly employed.

While plain radiographs can detect gross sinus disease, the large anatomical variation that can occur has made interpretation in this context very difficult. The advent of sinus endoscopy has reduced the requirement for plain radiographs, with CT or MRI now preferred.

Key points

- Always check the patient's name and age and date of the film
- Assess film quality. The mandible should be present on standard facial views
- Familiarise yourself with normal anatomical vascular markings and normal anatomical skull sutures, in order to recognise linear fractures.
- Trace McGrigor's lines to identify bony or soft tissue injuries
- Look for a dense white line, which may represent a depressed skull fracture
- Look for an air-fluid level in the sphenoid sinus, indicative of a base of skull fracture
- Look for soft tissue in the roof of the maxillary antrum. Cortical irregularity of the orbital floor is often absent in orbital 'blow out' fractures
- Regard the mandible as a bony ring. A second, more subtle mandibular fracture usually accompanies the more obvious one

References

National Institute for Health and Clinical Excellence (2007) *Head Injury: Triage, Assessment, Investigation and Early Management of Head Injury in Infants, Children and Adults. NICE Clinical Guideline 56*. National Collaborating Centre for Acute Care, London

CHAPTER 8

Cervical spine

Introduction

The cervical spine is particularly vulnerable to injury as it sits on the rigid thorax and provides flexible support for the head. Excessive flexion, rotation or compression may lead to bony or ligamentous damage and render the cervical cord susceptible to irreversible trauma. Whiplash injury from road traffic collisions is a frequent cause of attendance in emergency departments and often requires only symptomatic treatment. However, direct impact and loading of the head and neck, such as may result from falls or sporting accidents, may lead to significant spinal trauma.

The priority for managing patients who present to emergency departments is to identify those who have a bony cervical spine injury, and thereby prevent potentially unstable fractures from causing neurological damage. However the great majority of patients who have plain radiographs taken will not have a spinal fracture. So an important issue is how to decide which patients merit investigation and which can be clinically examined and discharged. If a cervical spine series is requested it is essential to know what to look for and what the potential pitfalls are in missing abnormalities. Fractures may be subtle and more often than not the patient is pinioned to a spinal board making interpretation more difficult still. A small but significant number of patients have injuries that are missed and the consequences may be catastrophic for both the patient and the doctor.

Departmental protocols take much of the anguish out of clinical decision making in these cases. However a systematic approach and a brief mental checklist will dramatically reduce the chances of a missed fracture on plain films.

Anatomy

There are seven cervical vertebrae which support the skull and articulate with the thoracic spine. The normal cervical vertebral alignment is gently lordotic – which may straighten due to muscle spasm following a spinal injury. The vertebral bodies are the load-bearing structures of the spine and are cushioned by the gelatinous intervertebral discs. The pedicles and laminae form the protective neural canal surrounding the spinal cord. The inferior articular process of each vertebra forms a facet joint with the superior articular process of the vertebra below. The cervical nerve roots, of which there are eight, pass through the intervertebral foraminae where they may be vulnerable to compression by an acute disc prolapse. The vertebral arteries pass cranially within the foramina transversaria to contribute to the posterior circulation of the brain.

The C1 (atlas) and C2 (axis) vertebrae are adapted to support the cranium as well as allowing stable rotational movement of the head. The vertebral body of C1 is fused with that of C2 below to form the odontoid peg. The peg articulates with the anterior arch of C1 at the median atlanto-axial joint and posterior movement towards the medulla is prevented by the strong transverse ligament (*Figure 8.1*). Sometimes the peg remains unfused with the body of C2 and forms a separate os odontoideum. The weight of the skull is borne by the lateral masses of C1 which form the atlanto-occiptal joints with the occipital condyles above and the lateral atlanto-axial joints with C2 below. The cervical spine is further stabilised by the anterior and posterior longitudinal ligaments, the interspinous ligaments and the ligamentum flavum.

Who needs imaging?

Cervical spine trauma is common but less than 2% attending an emergency department will have a clinically significant injury and most will only require conservative management. Avoiding indiscriminate radiographs will help to reduce exposure to medical ionizing radiation and may reduce costs and unnecessary delays. A number of guidelines have been suggested to rationalise the use of cervical radiographs and have been validated in clinical trials. If certain criteria are fulfilled (*Table 8.1*) then clinical assessment of the cervical spine may be performed without resorting to radiographs. If there is no bruising, tenderness or deformity and there is a full range of pain-free neck movement then no further investigations are required.

In patients who do not satisfy these criteria, lateral, anteroposterior (AP) and open-mouth radiographs are performed. However, between 10 and 20% of significant cervical spine injuries will be missed on plain radiographs. The majority of these will be due to poor radiographic technique or misinterpretation. If there is persisting clinical suspicion of a fracture, an abnormality is seen on plain radiographs, or the patient is unconscious then computed tomgraphy (CT) may be performed. With multidetector CT increasingly available the whole cervical spine may be

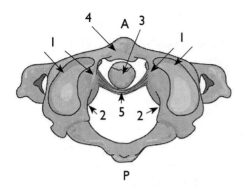

Figure 8.1. The first cervical vertebra articulates with the occiput above (1) and C2 below (2). The odontoid peg (3) articulates with the anterior arch (4) and is supported by the transverse ligament (5). A (anterior) and P (posterior).

Table 8.1. Criteria for clinical assessment of the cervical spine (British Trauma Society, 2003)

- Fully alert and orientated
- No head injury
- No sedative drugs or alcohol
- No neck pain, swelling or tenderness
- No neurological deficit
- No significant distracting injury

rapidly imaged at high resolution, and multiplanar reformats produced. However, CT is not routinely used as a first-line investigation to 'clear' the cervical spine and should be interpreted in conjunction with the plain radiographs and clinical findings.

Magnetic resonance imaging (MRI) has a role in cases when spinal cord injury, ligamentous damage or intervertebral disc prolapse is suspected. Its wide coverage may also demonstrate non-contiguous injuries.

Radiographs and how to read them

Plain radiographs are the usual first-line investigation for suspected cervical spine injuries. Most significant injuries will be apparent on the lateral view of the spine which forms part of the trauma series with chest and pelvic radiographs. It is important to assess the adequacy of the film which may have been taken in a sub-optimal situation with the patient immobilised on a spinal board and wearing a hard collar. It is unfortunate that the parts of the spine that are most vulnerable to injury are also those that are frequently obscured by other bones and soft tissues. Firstly, count the number of cervical vertebrae shown. The film is inadequate if the whole cervical spine from the occiput to the C7/T1 junction is not shown, especially as the latter level is vulnerable to injury due to the relative mobility of the neck compared to the thoracic spine. In some circumstances it may be possible to cautiously apply shoulder traction to reveal the lower cervical vertebrae. Altenatively, a 'swimmer's' view may be performed with one arm pulled down and the other arm elevated beside the head (*Figure 8.2*). Trauma obliques are performed less commonly but are used to demonstrate the posterior cervical elements and the alignment of C7/T1. These views will be less familiar to many and may require interpretation by an experienced person. Flexion and extension views of the cervical spine may be hazardous in the acute setting and are performed only under expert supervision.

The craniocervical junction should also be clearly seen on an adequate lateral radiograph. The width of the median atlanto-axial joint (pre-dental space) should not exceed 3mm in adults. The outline of each cervical vertebra should be scrutinised carefully to look for fractures, and the equal spacing of the intervertebral discs reviewed. Three lines may be drawn on the lateral radiograph to ensure normal alignment (*Figure 8.3*). The anterior spinal line extends from the anterior margin of C1 along the anterior borders of the vertebral bodies. The posterior spinal line passes behind the odontoid peg and along the posterior borders of the vertebral bodies. Lastly, the spinolaminar line forms a smooth curve where the laminae fuse at the base of the spinous process. The normal facet joints should also have a regular overlapping configuration. Finally, indirect evidence of a fracture may be provided by the presence of para-spinal swelling or haematoma. The soft tissues anterior to C1–C4 should be no more than 4mm, but below this up to a full width of a vertebral body is acceptable.

The anteroposterior (AP) projection is particularly helpful for identifying rotation of a vertebra such as in unifacetal dislocation (*Figure 8.4*). Again a line should be drawn down the spinous processes between each vertebra to establish this. Occasionally unilateral or bilateral cervical ribs may be seen arising from C7. The craniocervical junction is obscured by the mandible and skull base on the AP view. An open mouth 'peg view' is performed to demonstrate the odontoid peg and its relationship to the adjacent lateral masses (*Figure 8.5*). The lateral borders of the lateral masses should align with the vertebra below. The palette may cast a line across the peg (Mach effect) but this is distinguished from a fracture as it extends beyond the anatomical borders of the bones.

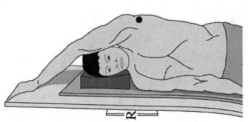

Figure 8.2. Positioning for the swimmer's view to radiograph the cervico-thoracic junction.

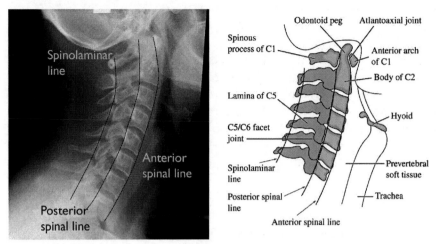

Figure 8.3. Normal lateral cervical radiograph showing three spinal lines.

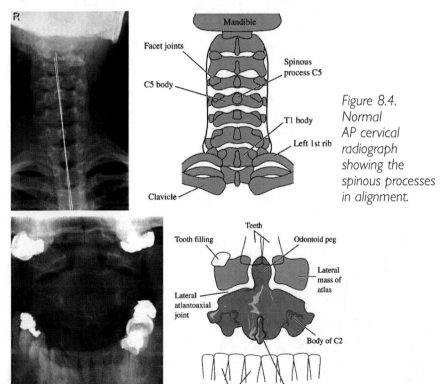

Figure 8.4. Normal AP cervical radiograph showing the spinous processes in alignment.

Figure 8.5. A normal 'peg' view taken through the open mouth. The teeth and palette are frequently projected over the peg and should not be mistaken for fractures. Lateral masses of C1 are shown on either side of the peg.

Table 8.2. Common interpretive errors

- Not being able to count the vertebrae correctly!
- Missing injuries at the cervico-thoracic junction
- Not looking for pre-vertebral swelling
- Inadequate peg view mimicking a fracture
- Assuming a normal x-ray means no injury

Common errors of interpretation are shown in *Table 8.2*.

Unstable injuries

While there is no universally accepted classification of what amounts to stable or unstable injuries it is reasonable to consider some injuries as having a higher risk of causing neurological damage. A three column model of the spine has been widely used for thoracolumbar injuries and is equally applicable to the cervical spine. The anterior column is composed of the anterior two thirds of the vertebral body and intervertebral disc, and the anterior longitudinal ligament. The middle column is composed of the posterior third of the vertebral body and intervertebral disc, and the posterior longitudinal ligament. The posterior column is comprised of the posterior elements formed by the pedicles, facet joints, transverse processes, laminae and the spinous process. Disruption of at least two columns is associated with instability. The following list of cervical spine injuries is not exhaustive but includes examples of important unstable fractures seen in clinical practice. Spinous process fractures (*Figure 8.6*), compression fractures (<25%), osteophyte fractures and fractures of the transverse process are considered stable.

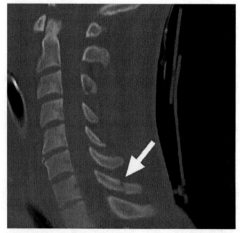

Figure 8.6. Sagittal reformat of a computed tomogram (CT) showing a fracture of the spinous process of C7 (arrow) (Clay shoveller's fracture).

Cervical spine injuries

Odontoid fracture

Fractures of the peg may occur at the tip of the dens, at its base or may extend into the vertebral body (*Figures 8.7 and 8.8*). The prevalence of spinal cord injury is high. There is also a risk of avascular necrosis of the dens with non-union of the fracture. The well-corticated os odontoideum may be mistaken for a fracture, and clinical correlation is important in this situation (*Figure 8.9*). Widening of the pre-dental space (atlanto-axial subluxation) is seen when there is rupture of the transverse ligament which may lead to cord compression.

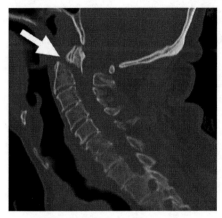

Figure 8.7. Sagittal reformat of a computed tomogram (CT) showing a fracture through the base of the dens (arrow).

Atlanto-occipital dissociation

Atlanto-occipital dissociation is a rare but severe injury which results in complete rupture of the craniocervical junction and is associated with life-threatening spinal cord damage.

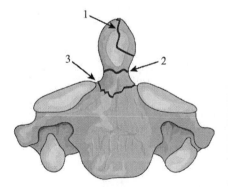

Figure 8.8. Odontoid fractures may be at the tip of the peg (1), across the base of the peg (2) or extend into the body of the vertebra (3).

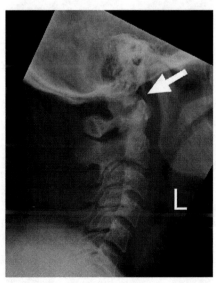

Figure 8.9. A lateral radiograph showing an os odontoideum (arrow).

Atlas fractures

C1 forms a ring and the stability of a fracture will depend on the point at which the fractures lie (*Figures 8.10, 8.11*). A fracture may cause lateral displacement of the lateral mass on the open-mouth peg view. An axial load may lead to the unstable Jefferson fracture where the bony ring is disrupted in four places.

Hangman's fracture

This is a hyperextension injury causing bilateral fractures through the pedicles of C2. It is usually evident on the lateral radiograph and may be associated with facet joint dislocation (*Figure 8.12*).

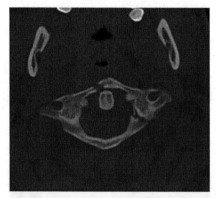

Figure 8.10. An axial computed tomogram (CT) demonstrating fractures of the C1 vertebra (atlas).

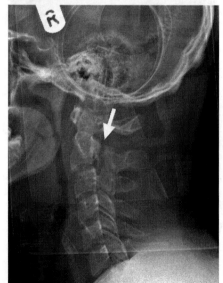

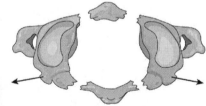

Figure 8.11. (above) A fracture of the atlas (C1) commonly breaks the ring into four fragments.

Figure 8.12. (left) A lateral radiograph demonstrating a Hangman's fracture of C2 (arrow).

Flexion teardrop fracture

Hyperflexion of the spine with an axial load may cause this severe and highly unstable injury. A triangular fragment of the antero-inferior vertebral body remains attached to the anterior longitudinal ligament with posterior displacement of the middle and posterior columns. This is invariably associated with spinal cord injury.

Burst fracture

A fall from a height may result in a compressive fracture of a vertebral body causing disruption of the anterior and middle columns. A CT is usually performed to assess the extent of neural canal narrowing by retropulsed bone. If there is greater than 25% loss of vertebral body height, retropulsion or neurological deficit the injury is unstable.

Bilateral facet joint dislocation

In this injury the facet joints dislocate antero-superiorly causing displacement of more than half the width of a vertebral body on the lateral radiograph (*Figures 8.13 and 8.14*). There is extensive disruption of ligamentous stability and a high incidence of spinal cord injury. A flexion-rotation injury is responsible for the stable injury of unilateral facet joint dislocation. This causes less anterior displacement on the lateral view, and the spinous process is rotated with respect the adjacent levels on the AP view (*Figure 8.15*).

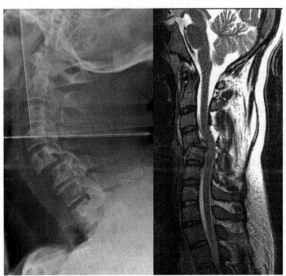

Figure 8.13. On the left is a lateral radiograph showing a bilateral facet joint dislocation. On the right is a sagittal T2-weighted magnetic resonance (MR) image, in a different patient, showing compression of the cervical cord.

97

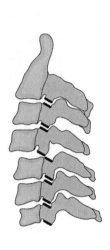

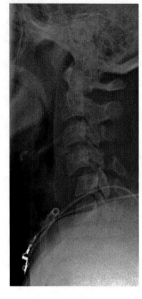

Figure 8.14. (far left) Bilateral facet joint dislocation leads to locked facets and requires traction to reduce them.
Figure 8.15. (left) A lateral radiograph showing unilateral facet joint dislocation, with subluxation on the other side.

Summary

Spinal injury is common and may have serious neurological consequences. However, not all patients require imaging and a clear evidence-based protocol should make decision making easier. Conversely, not all spinal injuries are evident on plain radiographs and further imaging should be sought if there is a high clinical suspicion. Recognition of fractures requires an active structured approach to interpreting radiographs.

Key points

- Use a risk assessment protocol
- Ensure lateral radiographs include C1/C2 and C7/T1
- Spinal injury in unconscious patients may require CT
- Always use a lightbox or workstation to review radiographs
- Have a systematic method of review
- Extra vigilance is needed in degenerate spines or osteoporosis
- Spinal cord injury can occur despite normal radiographs

References

British Trauma Society (2003) Guidelines for the initial management and assessment of spinal injury. Injury 34: 405-25

CHAPTER 9

Thoracolumbar spine

Introduction

Thoracolumbar vertebral trauma is a major cause of spinal cord injury. Such severe disruption invariably results from significant force, although fortunately it is relatively uncommon. However, more minor injuries are frequently encountered yet still may cause uneasiness in their assessment. Plain radiographs remain the first-line investigation, but interpretation can be difficult because of the variety of possible injuries, and their sometimes subtle appearances. Understanding of normal anatomy is key to avoiding errors in the management of these injuries. This chapter provides a systematic approach to interpreting thoracic and lumbar radiographs and describes the common conditions requiring these X-rays along with radiological signs.

Anatomy

The thoracolumbar spine is more stable than the cervical spine mainly due to the nature of the supporting ligaments, but also due to the intervertebral discs, facet joint alignment, the ribs and the paravertebral muscles. These ligaments include the anterior and posterior longitudinal ligaments, which support the vertebral bodies, and a posterior ligament complex consisting of the supraspinous ligaments, interspinous ligaments and ligamentum flavum (supporting the posterior bony elements). An intact posterior longitudinal ligament usually renders the spine stable. Stability is obtained at the expense of the range of movement, which is clearly inferior to that of the cervical spine. As a result, generally, large forces are required to cause disruption, and most commonly at the points where the spinal lordosis changes direction, i.e. the cervicothoracic junction (discussed in *Chapter 8*), the thoracolumbar junction and the lumbosacral junction. The spinal cord usually terminates at the lower L1 vertebral level (L3 at birth), although its meningeal coverings pass caudally into the sacral canal enveloping nerve roots termed the cauda equina. External to the meningeal coverings is a potential space termed the extradural (or epidural) space, which contains fat, blood vessels and the exiting nerve roots. In the thoracic spine this space is limited in capacity by the significant cord width and relatively narrow bony canal, hence making an injury more likely to impinge the cord. More caudally in the lumbar canal the bony width is wider, the cauda equina thinner and this potential space is more able to compensate for an unstable injury.

Developmental anatomy

The vertebral bodies develop from at least three ossification centres, which may not fuse dorsally resulting in spina bifida (usually lumbosacral in location), or fuse in abnormal fashion resulting in hemivertebrae or lumbarisation of the upper sacrum (incomplete fusion) or sacralisation at L5 (fusion of L5 to ala of sacrum).

Interpretation of thoracic and lumbar radiographs

Routine radiographs of the thoracolumbar spine include a minimum of the anteroposterior (AP) and lateral view. Additional oblique views may allow assessment of the intervertebral foramina, pedicles and facet joints but are rarely of use.

Systematic radiological assessment

- The patient's name, date of birth and date on the film should always be checked.
- **Film quality**: All five lumbar vertebrae and the sacrum should be visualised on both the AP and lateral views of the lumbar spine. Similarly all the thoracic vertebrae should be visualised on both the AP and lateral views of the thoracic spine.
- **Bone and joint alignment**: The lateral view should be examined first as pathology is more commonly seen on this. The anterior and posterior longitudinal lines should be smooth curves, with a direction change at the thoracolumbar junction. The posterior elements should also follow this curve although overlying ribs often obscure this in the thoracic spine (*Figure 9.1*). The sacrum should show a kyphosis, which smoothly continues from the normal lumbar lordosis (*Figure 9.2*). On the AP view, the spinous processes should align (*Figure 9.3*); if malaligned they may have rotated to the side of an injury. The paraspinal line should be closely applied to the vertebral bodies in the thoracic region, and the distance between the pedicles gradually increases in the lumbar region (from L1 to L5) (*Figure 9.4*). The facet joints should align on both views.

- **Bony density and margins**: The cortical surfaces of each of the vertebrae should be systematically examined for irregularities. Vertebral bodies and discs should be of uniform height, increasing in size caudally. However, the L5/S1 disc may be slightly narrower than that of the L4/L5 disc. As with any other bone, the cortices should be smooth and regular, and depressions or steps should be considered as suspicious for a fracture. Similarly loss of the normal trabecular pattern and overlapping of bone fragments may indicate a significant injury. Visualisation of the posterior elements of the upper thoracic vertebrae is often poor due to overlapping ribs and scapulae. Significant clinical concern in this area may be an indication for computed tomography.
- **Soft tissues**: Soft tissue swelling causing disruption of the paraspinal line or psoas shadow is seen best on the AP view, and may be present in association with a significant injury.

Common interpretative errors are listed in *Table 9.1*.

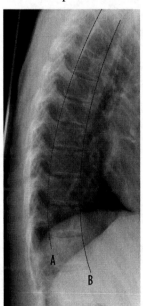 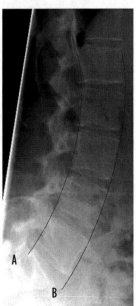

Figure 9.1. (left) A normal lateral thoracic spine radiograph showing normally aligned anterior longitudinal (line B), and posterior longitudinal (line A) lines. The normal smooth thoracic kyphosis is demonstrated. The posterior elements are also seen to follow this curve although overlying ribs obscure this to some extent. Figure 9.2. (right) A normal lateral lumbar spine radiograph showing normally aligned anterior longitudinal (line B), and posterior longitudinal (line A) lines. The normal smooth lumbar lordosis is demonstrated. The sacrum shows a kyphosis, which smoothly continues from the normal lumbar lordosis.

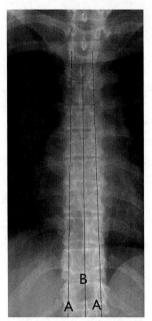 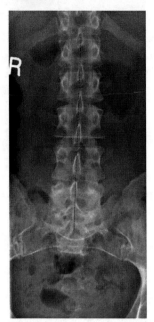

Figure 9.3. (left) A normal AP thoracic spine radiograph, showing normally aligned spinous processes (line B) and pedicles (line A). If malaligned they may have rotated to the side of an injury.

Figure 9.4. (right) A normal AP lumbar spine radiograph, showing normally aligned spinous processes (line). The distance between the pedicles gradually increases (from L1 to L5).

- Avulsed endplate fractures can be subtle and may be associated with a significant injury. The bony cortices of each vertebra should be carefully assessed
- A widened interpedicular space may be the only sign of a fracture on the AP radiograph so should be carefully assessed
- Axial compression injuries may result in a loss of disc height with sometimes no obvious fracture. The disc may be retropulsed into the canal causing neurological compromise. Disc heights should be carefully assessed in injuries of this type
- Isolated transverse and spinous process fractures are common, but they may be subtle. They can be associated with other severe injuries. They may require a bright light to be discovered or rewindowing on an X-ray workstation/monitor

Spinal trauma

Flexion injuries

The majority of fractures result from flexion injuries, usually causing anterior compression (wedging) and posterior distraction (*Figure 9.5*), although lateral flexion will result in lateral compression. This occurs most commonly at T12 to L2 in adults, and at T4 to T5 in children. If posterior vertebral height is maintained, these fractures are usually stable as the posterior longitudinal ligaments are usually intact. If the force is sufficient however, there can be disruption of the posterior ligamentous complex, and multiple vertebrae may be significantly wedged with associated loss of disc height leading to an unstable injury (*Figure 9.6*).

The flexion-distraction injury or 'Chance fracture' occurs usually due to restraint by a seatbelt. This usually occurs at L1–3, is frequently unstable and is associated with other visceral injuries. It consists of a horizontal fracture through the body, pedicle and posterior elements (*Figure 9.7*).

Flexion-rotation injuries are unusual but extremely unstable usually resulting in neurological impairment. The characteristic findings are rotation between adjacent vertebrae and vertebral dislocation. Associated fractures are common.

Shearing injuries

These severe injuries usually result from a force causing anterior or posterior displacement of a vertebra with respect to the one below, by often more than 25%. This may involve disruption of all of the intervertebral ligaments and is highly unstable.

Hyperextension injuries

These injuries are rare but can occur if the patient falls and hyperextends over an object. These injuries are more frequent in patients with ankylosing spondylitis and can occur with more minor trauma. Radiographic findings include widening of the anterior part of the disc space, an avulsion fracture of the anterior superior vertebral corner, and occasionally a posterior arch fracture in severe cases.

Axial compression injuries

This type of injury usually results from a fall from a height, and causes the vertebral bodies to compress the intervertebral disc, which may herniate

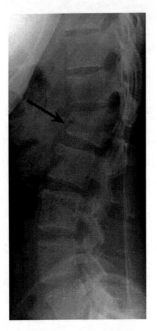 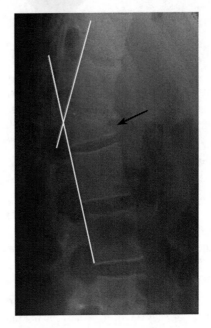

Figure 9.5. (left) A lateral lumbar spine radiograph showing an acute anterior wedge fracture of the L1 vertebral body, as visualised by loss of anterior vertebral body height (arrow). The majority of spinal fractures result from flexion injuries, usually causing anterior compression (wedging).

Figure 9.6. (right) A lateral lumbar spine radiograph showing an acute anterior wedge fracture of a lumbar vertebral body (arrow). The force is sufficient however, to have caused disruption of the posterior longitudinal ligament, as indicated by malalignment of the posterior aspect of the vertebral body with respect to the adjacent levels (lines). This is a potentially unstable injury.

posteriorly into the canal, and may disrupt the longitudinal ligaments. In more extreme cases the vertebral bodies themselves 'burst' from within, with variable displacement of the fragments (*Figure 9.8*). These injuries can occur from T4 to L5, although most commonly at L1. Radiographic findings include a widened interpedicular distance, anterior wedging and a vertical fracture line (*Figure 9.9*). Retropulsed endplate fractures are also seen. These injuries can be unstable, particularly if there are rotational components to the mechanism of injury, or compression of more than 50% has occurred. Neurological injury and other associated fractures are frequent.

Isolated transverse and spinous process fractures are not uncommon and usually result from direct trauma. They may be subtle and require a bright light to be discovered, and although they may be of no significance they can be associated with other injuries. At T1–2 and L4–5 they are associated with injuries to the brachial and lumbosacral plexuses respectively.

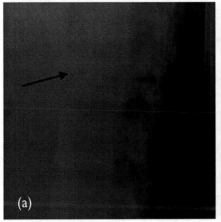

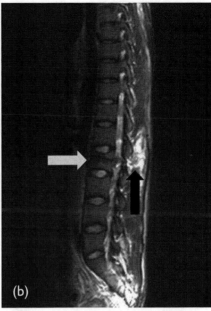

Figure 9.7. A patient with a flexion-distraction injury or 'Chance fracture' of the L2 vertebral body. This is frequently unstable and is associated with other visceral injuries. It consists of a horizontal fracture through the vertebral body, pedicle and posterior elements. (a) A lateral lumbar spine radiograph showing a horizontal fracture of the vertebral body (arrow). (Reproduced with permission from Harvey et al. (2005) Self Assessment Cases in Surgical Imaging. Oxford University Press). (b) A sagittal T2-weighted magnetic resonance image showing the L2 body fracture (white arrow). The injury to the posterior elements is appreciated as shown by high signal soft tissue abnormality (black arrow).

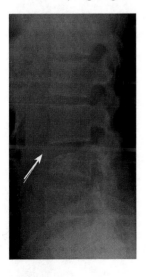

Figure 9.8. A lateral lumbar spine radiograph showing an acute 'burst' fracture of the L3 vertebral body. This injury has occurred due to a fall from a height and has caused the vertebral body to compress the intervertebral disc. The vertebral body itself has 'burst' from within, with anterior wedging and displacement of the fragments (arrow).

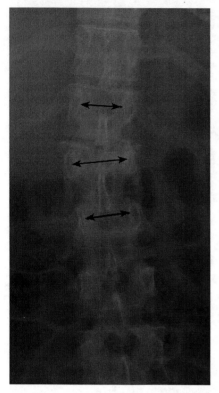

Figure 9.9. An AP lumbar radiograph showing an acute 'burst' fracture of the L1 vertebral body. There is slight malalignment and a widened interpedicular distance at this level when compared to the adjacent spinal levels (arrows).

Non-traumatic presentations

Many patients present to the emergency department with non-traumatic back pain and although this may be disabling, in the absence of significant neurology, the vast majority of these patients will not have an urgent clinical problem. They may have one or multiple osteoporotic crush fractures (*Figure 9.10*), or they may have varying degrees of degenerative disease, or non-traumatic spondylolisthesis (*Figure 9.11*) perhaps with secondary nerve root irritation and associated muscular spasm. Their pain may indeed be referred from somewhere else. However, occasionally back pain can be due to a serious cause such as bony metastatic disease or myelomatous infiltration, or a spinal infection such as an osteomyelitis or discitis (*Figure 9.12*). This should be suspected clinically on a careful and thorough history and examination.

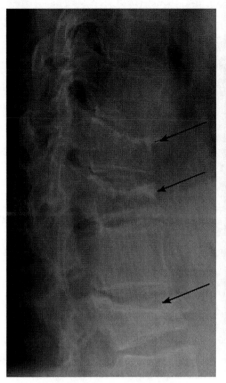

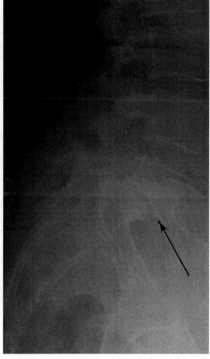

Figure 9.10. A lateral thoracic spine radiograph showing the loss of vertebral body height at multiple spinal levels. The bones are generally lucent in keeping with osteoporosis and the fractures are hence 'non-traumatic' osteoporotic crush fractures (arrows).

Figure 9.11. A lateral lumbar spine radiograph showing vertebral body malalignment at the L5–S1 level, indicating a grade 2 spondylolisthesis (arrow). Spondylolisthesis is graded by measuring how much of the vertebral body has slipped forward over the body beneath it. Grade 1 is a slip of less than 25%, grade 2 is 25–50%, grade 3 is 50–75%, grade 4 is 75–100%. Although this can occur secondary to significant trauma, degenerative disease can also cause this (as in this case), particularly at this site.

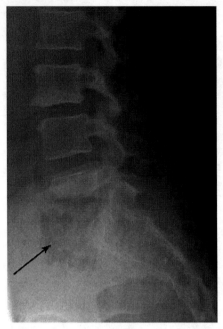

Figure 9.12. A lateral lumbar spine radiograph showing an acute discitis. There is gas overlying the L5–S1 disc space, with associated destruction of the adjacent vertebral endplates (arrow). This has occurred secondarily to a systemic infection with staphylococcus aureus.

Key points

- Always check the name and age and date of the film.
- Assess film quality, ensuring all the vertebrae are visualised.
- Assess the alignment of the thoracic and lumbar spine, particularly with respect to the change in curvature at the thoracolumbar and sacrolumbar junctions.
- Assess each vertebra in turn for height, shape, bony cortices and interpedicular distance. Allow for slight widening of interpedicular distances from L1–5.
- Assess the intervertebral disc spaces, facet joints and paravertebral soft tissues for uniformity.

CHAPTER 10

Pelvis and hip

Introduction

The angulation of the neck of the femur acts as a flying buttress to transfer the compressive stresses of the pelvis onto the laterally placed femoral shafts. Excessive loads borne by the lower limbs will be transmitted upwards and will often cause fracturing of this vulnerable structure. Fractured neck of femur is an important cause of morbidity and mortality in the elderly. For medical and social reasons falls are common in this age group, a problem that is compounded by the presence of age-related osteoporosis. Leg shortening and external rotation of the hip are the classical findings but are not invariably present. While the findings of a fracture on plain radiographs are usually straightforward there are potential pitfalls in interpretation. In certain cases specialised imaging techniques may be required to confirm the existence of a fracture. Fractures of the pubic rami are also frequently seen among the elderly, although the treatment is often conservative.

Other pelvic fractures are most commonly encountered in those involved in high impact trauma and particularly road traffic accidents. Unstable injuries may require orthopaedic surgery and there is an associated risk of neurological, vascular and urogenital trauma. The pattern of injuries is dictated by the solid ring structure of the pelvis and sacrum with weak-points at the sacroiliac joints and pubic symphysis.

Bony anatomy

The pelvis forms a bony ring consisting of two innominate bones and the sacrum which is reinforced by ligaments (*Figure 10.1*). Force applied to one area will result in disruption elsewhere in the ring. The innominate bone comprises the ilium, ischium, and pubis. Posteriorly the innominate bones articulate with the sacrum at the sacroiliac joints and anteriorly at the pubic symphysis. The ilium forms the iliac crests superiorly; the pubis forms the superior and inferior pubic rami around the obturator foramen; and the ischium forms the lesser and greater sciatic notches and the projection of the ischial tuberosity. The ossification centres for these bones meet at the triradiate cartilage. It is here that the acetabulum forms a synovial ball-and-socket joint with the spherical femoral head connected by the ligamentum teres. The neck is set at an angle of 125 degrees to the shaft. The trochanteric crest joins the lateral greater trochanter and the medial lesser trochanter.

The blood supply to the femoral head is of great importance in determining the vascular deficits resulting from a fracture. The femoral head receives its blood from vessels that pass along the joint capsule and are reflected proximally in the retinaculum (*Figure 10.2*). There is only a negligible centrifugal blood supply via the ligamentum teres. Arteries also pass upwards from the femoral diaphysis to supply the neck of femur. A fracture in the inter-trochanteric plane still allows blood to reach the femoral head from the retinaculum. However, an intracapsular fracture at the subcapital or transcervical level will disrupt both the retinacular and diaphyseal blood supply and lead to avascular necrosis of the femoral head.

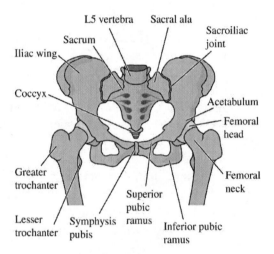

Figure 10.1. Pelvic anatomy.

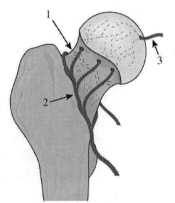

Figure 10.2. An intracapsular fracture of the neck of femur (1) may lead to avascular necrosis of the femoral head. The main blood supply arises from an arterial ring below the capsular margin (2) with only an inconsistent supply from above via the ligamentum teres (3).

Imaging

The mainstay of imaging remains the plain radiograph. The anteroposterior (AP) pelvic view is part of the trauma series of images along with the lateral cervical spine and chest X-ray. Patients lie supine and the cassette is placed underneath them. A lateral view may also provide additional valuable information and is performed with flexion of the affected hip. Diagnostic quality may be limited in obese patients and using a bright light or re-windowing on a workstation is often necessary. Other views are now rarely required in adults. Computed tomography (CT) is performed in cases of unstable pelvic injuries in which orthopaedic surgery is contemplated or if there is suspected trauma to the pelvic viscera. Three dimensional reconstructions may be helpful in planning reconstructive surgery. CT or fluoroscopic cysto-urethrography may be needed to exclude bladder perforation or disruption to the urethra.

Impacted femoral neck fractures may be difficult to appreciate on early radiographs. A coronal magnetic resonance imaging study readily demonstrates discontinuity of bone marrow and localised oedema in these cases (*Figure 10.3*). Magnetic resonance imaging (MRI) is also a sensitive test for evaluating the presence of avascular necrosis.

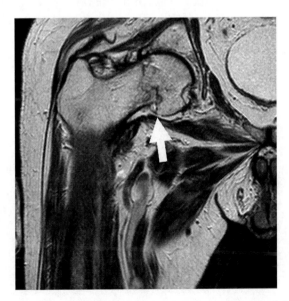

Figure 10.3. Coronal T2-weighted magnetic resonance image of the right hip. The wavy dark band (arrow) demonstrates an impacted femoral neck fracture that was not seen on plain radiographs.

Tips on interpretation

Many injuries will be readily apparent but a systematic approach will help to avoid missing fractures. Carefully scrutinise the whole pelvic ring. If one fracture is seen then another fracture or dislocation is usually associated with it. Ensure that the sacro-iliac joints are not widened or asymmetrical, or that there is not diastasis of the pubic symphysis. Review the bones forming the obturator foramina, again looking for complementary fractures. Acetabular fractures are essential to recognise and the film should be inspected for continuity of the ilio-pectineal and ilio-ischial lines (*Figure 10.4*). The sacrum should not be overlooked and any symmetry of the arcuate lines of the sacral foramina should raise the suspicion of a fracture. The appearance of the coccyx is variable and injuries are not clinically important.

Femoral neck fractures are frequently displaced and clearly seen, however some fractures are only revealed by looking for subtle findings. Look carefully at the trabecular pattern of the femoral neck to ensure it is not disrupted. Also review the bone cortex for a breach or the dense transverse line of an impacted fracture (*Figure 10.5*). The curve of the lower border of the superior pubic ramus and the inferior aspect of the neck of the femur should form a smooth arc (Shenton's line) which becomes discontinuous following a fracture. The medial half of the femoral head is projected over the posterior acetabular rim in the normally located hip.

Common errors of interpretation are shown in *Table 10.1*.

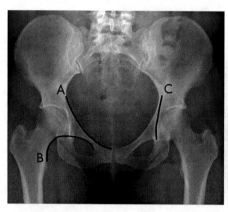

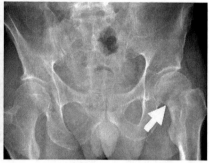

Figure 10.4. AP view of the normal pelvis. Iliopectineal line (line A), Shenton's line (line B), ilio-ischial line (line C).

Figure 10.5. The impacted subcapital femoral neck fracture is revealed by a dense transverse band (arrow).

Table 10.1. Common interpretive errors

- Missing fractures of the sacral foramina and sacro-iliac joints
- Mistaking epiphyseal lines or the superimposed rim of the acetabulum for neck of femur fractures
- Failing to consider vascular or urological injury after pelvic fractures

Important injuries

Anterior-posterior compression pelvic fractures

These injuries are the result of force applied directly to the anterior or posterior aspects of the pelvis such as in a head-on road traffic collision. They lead to widening or disruption of the pubic symphysis and sacroiliac joints. There may be variable rupture of the sacrotuberous and sacrospinous ligaments which determine the stability of the injury (*Figure 10.6*). Obturator ring fractures may also be associated.

Vertical shear pelvic fracture

The mechanism of this injury is an axial load on the pelvis most commonly transmitted through the lower limb such as in a fall from a height. This manifests itself as vertical displacement of the hemipelvis compared to the contralateral side (*Figure 10.7*). In the anterior pelvis pubic rami fractures are observed (*Figure 10.8*), while posteriorly the sacrum is fractured or there is sacroiliac joint diastasis. Alternatively a fracture of the iliac wing may occur.

Lateral compression pelvic fractures

These are the most commonly seen type of pelvic ring fractures and occur when there is direct force to the lateral aspect of the pelvis such as in a side impact collision (*Figure 10.9*). Complex obturator ring fractures are invariably present. An ipsilateral sacral compression fracture or iliac wing fracture are commonly associated. The most unstable form comprises a lateral compression injury on the side of the impact and a contralateral anterior-posterior compression fracture (windswept pelvis).

Avulsion fractures

Fractures of the apophyses at the site of tendon insertions are usually seen in

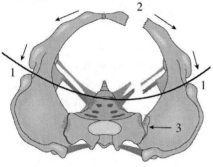

Figure 10.6. In an AP compression fracture the iliac spines (1) are forced outwards. Anterior fractures (2) at the pubic ramus or symphysis pubis occur, as well as posterior fractures around the sacroiliac joints (3). These are described as 'open-book' injuries.

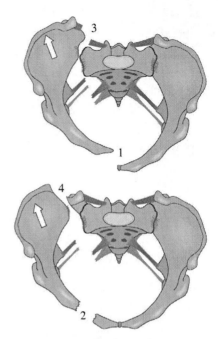

Figure 10.7. In a vertical shear fracture the pelvic ring is disrupted anteriorly at the pubic symphysis (1) or pubic rami (2), and posteriorly there is dislocation of the sacroiliac joint (3) or a fracture of the posterior iliac spine (4).

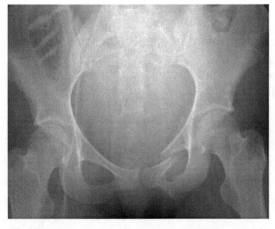

Figure 10.8. A vertical shear fracture. The inferior and superior pubic rami fractures were accompanied by a sacral fracture (not shown).

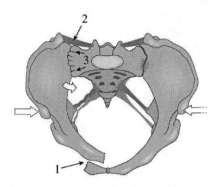

Figure 10.9. A lateral compression fracture results in fractures of the pubic rami (1). The posterior sacro-iliac ligaments (2) remain intact with compression fractures of the anterior margin of the sacroiliac joint (3).

young atheletes, especially footballers and gymnasts. The avulsed fragment of bone has a typical location on the pelvic ring (*Figure 10.10*). Common fracture sites and the tendon insertions include the anterior superior iliac spine (sartorius), anterior inferior iliac spine (rectus femoris), ischial tuberosity (hamstrings) and the pubic tubercle (adductors).

Acetabular fractures

Functionally the pelvis comprises an anterior pelvic column (iliac wing, superior pubic ramus and anterior wall of the acetabulum) and a posterior pelvic column (posterior ilium, posterior and medial acetabular walls and the ischium). Acetabular fractures may involve the walls of the acetabulum and the pelvic columns (*Figure 10.11*). The most common injury is a fracture of both columns in which the free-floating acetabulum is displaced

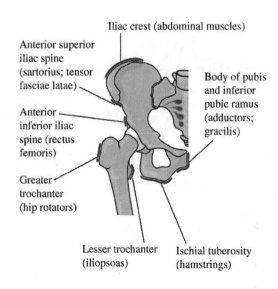

Iliac crest (abdominal muscles)

Anterior superior iliac spine (sartorius; tensor fasciae latae)

Anterior inferior iliac spine (rectus femoris)

Greater trochanter (hip rotators)

Body of pubis and inferior pubic ramus (adductors; gracilis)

Lesser trochanter (iliopsoas)

Ischial tuberosity (hamstrings)

Figure 10.10. The location of avulsion fractures around the pelvis.

medially (*Figure 10.12*). The 'spur-sign' represents the part of the ilium that remains attached to the sacrum. The iliopectineal line, from the sciatic notch to the superior pubic ramus, is the landmark for the anterior column, and the ilio-ischial line, from the sciatic notch inferiorly into the teardrop, indicates continuity of the posterior column.

Hip dislocation

Posterior dislocations are the most common injury by far and are frequently caused by the knee striking the dashboard in a road traffic collision. The femoral head may be fractured against the acetabulum and the ligamentum teres avulsed. On the frontal pelvic X-ray the femoral head is displaced superiorly and laterally. In the rarer anterior dislocation the femoral head is generally projected over the obturator foramen.

Fractured neck of femur

This is the most commonly encountered injury. Careful examination of the femoral neck, continuity of the trabeculae and integrity of Shenton's line should be ensured in each film. The level of the fracture should be documented as this reflects the potential for the development of avascular necrosis (*Figure 10.13*), as well as whether the fracture is displaced (*Figures 10.5, 10.14, 10.15*). Stress fractures occur over time and may be compressive, starting on the inferior cortex, or tension, starting on the superior cortex.

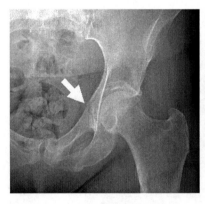

Figure 10.11. A pelvic fracture disrupting the iliopectineal line.

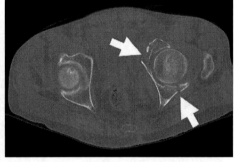

Figure 10.12. An axial computed tomogram of the pelvis demonstrating fractures of the pelvic columns and acetabular walls (arrows).

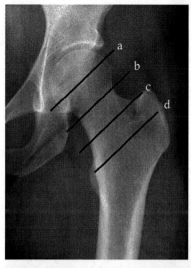

Figure 10.13. The level of the fractured neck of femur determines the likelihood of avascular necrosis developing. (A) Subcapital, (B) transcervical, (C) basi-cervical, (D) intertrochanteric. A subcapital fracture has an 80% chance of avascular necrosis of the proximal femoral head.

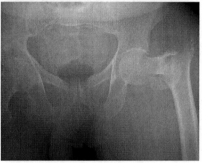

Figure 10.14. An intertrochanteric fracture of the neck of femur.

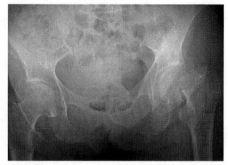

Figure 10.15. A basi-cervical fracture of the neck of femur.

Summary

Pelvic fractures are complex injuries but an understanding of functional anatomy makes the radiological appearances more understandable. While these are usually seen in the context of high-impact trauma, femoral neck fractures are a common presentation in the elderly following a fall. Systematic review of the film, with a bright light if necessary, is needed to avoid missing subtle injuries.

Key Points

- Pelvic ring fractures are frequently multiple
- Sacroiliac joints and pubic symphysis may be involved

- Some injuries are unstable and may lead to trauma of the intra-pelvic viscera
- Femoral neck fractures are common but may be subtle
- Document the level of femoral neck fracture and the degree of displacement

CHAPTER 11

Knee

Introduction

The knee is particularly susceptible to traumatic injury due to the variety of compressive, load-bearing and rotational forces that may act upon it. Injuries may be the result of high-impact trauma, such as falls from a height or road traffic accidents, or due to low-velocity sporting injuries. They may be associated with signific ant complications such as vascular injury, compartment syndrome, bony non-union, avascular necrosis and osteoarthritis. The majority of fractures are visible on plain radiographs although detectable injuries are sometimes subtle. Simple guidelines are available in order to help decide which injuries do not require investigation with radiographs.

Anatomy

The shaft of the distal femur expands into the medial and lateral femoral condyles separated by an intercondylar fossa. The patella is a sesamoid bone within the quadriceps tendon and lies in the V-shaped trochlear groove of the anterior articular surface of the distal femur. Patellar dislocation usually occurs across the shallower lateral articular facet. Occasionally the patella is bipartite with an unfused superolateral ossification centre. The inferior articular surfaces of the femur articulate with the central tibial condyles while the peripheral portions are supported by the medial and lateral menisci. The broad tibial plateau tapers into the shaft distally. On its anterior surface lies the tibial tuberosity onto which inserts the patellar tendon. The anterior and posterior cruciate ligaments form a cross-shape between the inward-facing surfaces of the femoral condyles and the tibial intercondylar area (*Figure 11.1*). Along with the medial and lateral collateral ligaments these structures help to stabilise movements of the knee.

The popliteal fossa is a space formed at the back of the knee. It contains the popliteal artery and vein, and is traversed by the tibial nerve. The common peroneal nerve passes adjacent to the biceps femoris tendon and winds around the neck of the fibula. The suprapatellar bursa is a potential space that lies between the suprapatellar and pre-femoral fat pads. It usually

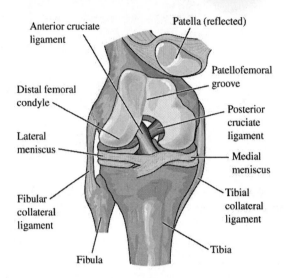

Anterior cruciate ligament

Patella (reflected)

Distal femoral condyle

Patellofemoral groove

Posterior cruciate ligament

Lateral meniscus

Medial meniscus

Fibular collateral ligament

Tibial collateral ligament

Fibula

Tibia

11.1. The major ligaments of the knee.

communicates with the knee joint space and can fill with effusion or haemorrhage following trauma.

Imaging

The mainstay of skeletal imaging is the plain radiograph. A minimum of two views are always required which include the anteroposterior (AP) and lateral projections. In the setting of trauma a horizontal beam lateral (HBL) view is taken with the patient positioned supine. Following a fracture haemorrhagic marrow may fill the suprapatellar bursa (*Figure 11.2a, b*). The fat layers on top of the blood to form a lipohaemarthrosis which is demonstrated on a HBL view. A tunnel view of the intercondylar notch may reveal fractures of the tibial spines or intra-articular loose bodies. Skyline views are used to demonstrate the patello-femoral joint in profile.

Computed tomography (CT) is used in selected cases of complex trauma which may require surgical reconstruction. In particular the degree of depression of tibial plateau fractures may be difficult to assess on plain films alone. MRI demonstrates the menisci, tendons and ligaments around the knee and is used to assess soft tissue injuries non-invasively. Bone oedema

---

Table 11.1. Common interpretive errors

- Not looking for a lipohaemarthrosis
- Mistaking a bipartite patella for a fracture
- Mistaking an unfused tibial tubercle for an avulsion fracture

---

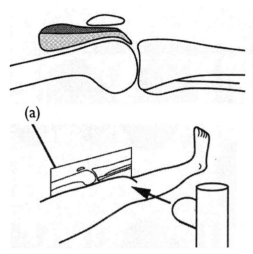

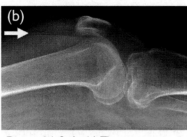

Figure 11.2 (a, b) The positioning of the patient for a horizontal beam lateral film allows a fat-blood fluid level of a lipohaemarthrosis to be seen (arrow). This indicates an intra-articular fracture.

and avascular necrosis are also readily visualised. Ultrasound has a role in evaluating tendinopathy, fluid collections and synovial disease.

Common errors of interpretation are shown in *Table 11.1*.

Who needs an X-ray?

The majority of knee radiographs are normal. As with other extremity X-rays the use of decision-making protocols have been widely adopted to reduce the number of negative examinations. The Ottawa knee rules (Stiel et al, 1997) reduce the number of normal radiographs by up to a third with no missed fractures found at follow-up. If at least one of these criteria applies (*Table 11.2*) following an acute knee injury, then routine X-rays should be performed.

In the case of severe or multiple trauma it should be remembered that the standard acute trauma life support protocol should be adopted, and the patient stabilised before imaging extremity fractures. Knee dislocation with signs of vascular impairment should be reduced without delaying for radiographs.

Table 11.2. The Ottawa knee rules for obtaining plain radiographs

- Age 55 years or older
- Tenderness at the head of the fibula
- Isolated tenderness of the patella
- Inability to flex to 90 degrees
- Inability to weight bear both immediately and in the emergency department (take 4 steps)

Knee injuries

Patella fractures and dislocation

Fractures of the patella are relatively common and often result from direct blunt trauma or from forceful quadriceps contraction (*Figure 11.3*). Transverse fractures are most commonly seen and usually occur across the middle of the patella (*Figure 11.4*). Comminuted fractures may occur and are sometimes stellate in appearance. Osteochondral fractures, comprising a fragment of cartilage and bone, occur more commonly in adolescents and may give rise to loose intra-articular bodies. A potential pitfall is mistaking a bipartite patella for a fracture. This normal variant can be distinguished by its well-corticated margin, which is usually in the supero-lateral quadrant (*Figure 11.5*).

Patella dislocations usually displace laterally and spontaneously reduce. Recurrent dislocations may be associated with developmental abnormalities of the patella and trochlear groove. Traumatic dislocations are associated with soft-tissue injuries and osteochondral fractures.

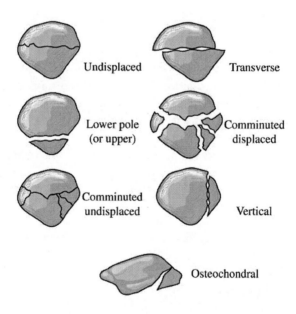

Undisplaced

Transverse

Lower pole (or upper)

Comminuted displaced

Comminuted undisplaced

Vertical

Osteochondral

Figure 11.3. The common types of patella fracture.

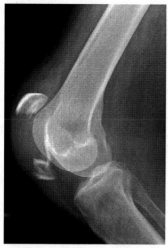

Figure 11.4. A lateral knee radiograph showing a widely displaced transverse fracture of the patella.

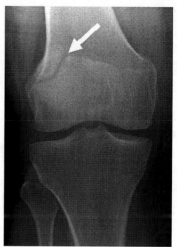

Figure 11.5. A frontal knee radiograph demonstrates a bipartite patella with an unfused ossification centre in the superolateral quadrant (arrow).

Femoral condyle fracture

Most fractures of the femoral condyles result from high impact trauma, although in the elderly a fall onto a flexed knee may be sufficient. Fractures may be extra-articular or involve one or both condyles. Additional injuries may occur to the femoral neck, shaft or acetabulum and surrounding ligaments. Radiographs should therefore include the pelvis, femur and knee. Minimally displaced condylar fractures may be easily missed and the frontal and lateral views should be carefully examined. Fractures may be comminuted and intra-articular extension should be noted.

Tibial plateau fracture

These injuries result from a lateral force on the knee joint combined with axial loading (*Figure 11.6*). The location of the fracture depends on the degree of knee flexion. A typical mechanism is a pedestrian being struck by the bumper of a car. There may be associated soft tissue injuries. Tears of the medial collateral ligament and the anterior cruciate may complicate lateral plateau fractures. Alternatively, tears of the lateral collateral or cruciate ligaments may accompany medial plateau injuries. High velocity injuries may lead to neurovascular damage and compartment syndrome.

The key finding on the plain radiographs is depression of the tibial plateau (*Figure 11.7*). On the normal frontal view the femoral condyles and upper tibia are in alignment. In a tibial plateau fracture the tibial margin is displaced so there is a step at the level of the knee joint. A perpendicular line drawn at the most lateral margin of the femur should not have more than 5mm of tibial plateau beyond it. The degree of displacement and comminution of the fragments should be noted. Computed tomography (CT) is often required for surgical planning to accurately assess the extent of articular depression (*Figure 11.8*). Magnetic resonance imaging (MRI) demonstrates meniscal and ligamentous ruptures and sprains, as well as post-traumatic bone oedema.

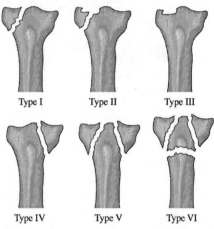

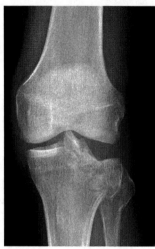

Figure 11.6. Tibial plateau fractures are classified using the Schatzker system. Type I: Lateral split; Type II: lateral split/depressed fracture; Type III: isolated lateral depression; Type IV: medial split; Type V: medial and lateral split; Type VI: medial and lateral split with diaphyseal-metaphyseal dissociation.

Figure 11.7. A frontal knee radiograph showing a comminuted fracture of the lateral tibial plateau extending into the tibial spines. The head of the fibula is also fractured.

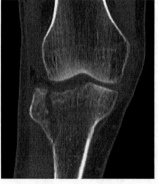

Figure 11.8. A coronal reformat of a knee computed tomogram (CT). This allows the extent of articular depression in a tibial plateau fracture to be accurately assessed.

Segond fracture

The Segond injury is a small avulsion fracture of the lateral tibia just distal to the plateau (*Figure 11.9*). This results from an injury with internal rotation which puts excessive stress on the lateral capsular ligament. Although the fracture appears minor it is commonly associated with rupture of the anterior cruciate and injury to the collateral ligaments.

Tibial spine fracture

Fractures of the tibial spine (or intercondylar eminence) are relatively rare. They nearly always involve the anterior spine and most commonly occur in children falling from a bicycle. They are associated with injuries to the anterior cruciate ligament.

Tibial tubercle fracture

Fractures to the tibial tubercle often occur in adolescence prior to growth plate fusion. The mechanism is typically related to jumping during forceful quadriceps contraction. The fracture plane involves the proximal tibial epiphysis and may extend to the articular surface of the knee. The fractures are usually apparent on the standard lateral radiograph and the fracture fragment is often displaced superiorly. In Osgood-Schlatter disease chronic microtrauma to the tibial tuberosity may produce a partial avulsion fracture and new bone formation.

It is important to be familiar with the normal appearance of the unfused tibial tubercle to avoid mistaking this for a fracture.

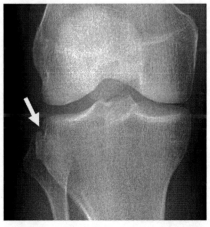

Figure 11.9. A frontal knee radiograph showing a Segond avulsion fracture (arrow). This is frequently associated with an anterior cruciate ligament rupture.

125

Knee dislocation

The mechanism of injury may be a high velocity impact, such as a road accident, or low velocity during a sporting injury. The dislocation is described by the position of the tibia relative to the femur and may be anterior, posterior, medial, lateral or rotatory. Further classification of the injury is made by the associated ligamentous damage sustained. Generally one or both of the cruciate ligaments are torn, but rarely they may remain intact. Avulsion fractures are also frequently seen. Vascular injury to the popliteal vessels may occur and prompt reduction is required.

Proximal tibio-fibular joint dislocation

Sudden plantar flexion with an inverted foot and a flexed knee may result in antero-lateral dislocation of the proximal tibio-fibular joint. On the anteroposterior radiograph the fibular head is displaced laterally and there is widening of the interosseous gap. On the lateral view the fibular head appears displaced anteriorly. Posteromedial and superior dislocations occur less commonly.

Conclusion

Knee injuries are common but most do not require X-rays. Conversely, some significant injuries may appear as quite subtle findings on radiographs and be associated with ligamentous damage.

Key points

- Use a protocol to decide who needs an X-ray
- Look for a lipohaemarthrosis on the lateral view
- Review areas are the femoral condyles, tibial plateau and around the proximal fibula
- Ligamentous injury may occur despite the absence of a fracture
- Normal variants and unfused epiphyses may be mistaken for fractures

Reference

Stiel IG, Wells GA, Hoag RH et al (1997) Implementation of the Ottawa Knee Rule for the use of radiography in acute knee injuries. *JAMA* **278**: 2075-79

CHAPTER 12

Ankle and foot

Introduction

Lower limb trauma is extremely common, with ankle and foot radiographs frequently simultaneously requested, as clinically it is often difficult to elucidate the exact site of trauma. Careful clinical assessment is imperative to minimise the amount of unnecessary radiographs. Plain radiographs remain the first-line investigation, but interpretation can be difficult because of the variety of possible injuries, and their sometimes subtle appearances. Understanding of normal anatomy is key to avoiding errors in the management of these injuries. This chapter provides a systematic approach to interpreting ankle and foot radiographs and describes the common conditions requiring these X-rays along with radiological signs.

Adult anatomy

The ankle joint consists of three bones and multiple ligaments. The distal fibula and tibia articulate with each other, joined by an interosseous membrane or syndesmosis. Posterior and anterior tibiofibular ligaments strengthen this joint. The talus articulates with both distal fibula and tibia (also termed medial and lateral malleoli). Lateral and medial collateral ligament complexes connect the malleoli to the talus and also calcaneum. The talus is locked between the malleoli in extreme dorsiflexion, with no movement possible in this position. The posterior aspect of the tibia is also termed the posterior malleolus.

The foot is divided into three areas; the hindfoot, the midfoot and the forefoot. The hindfoot consists of the talus and calcaneum, which articulate at the subtalar joint. The remaining tarsal bones make up the midfoot, with the metatarsals and phalanges comprising the forefoot. Numerous ligaments link the multiple bones, but one of the most clinically important ligaments is Lisfranc's ligament, which extends from the medial cuneiform to the base of the second metatarsal.

Developmental anatomy

The developing ankle and foot can have numerous accessory ossification centres, although the commonest is the os trigonum which is posterior to the talus. This is present in up to 25% of the population but is commonly mistaken for a fracture. Other ossification centres are less common but typically are regular and well corticated, and should be distinguished from fractures.

Interpretation of ankle and foot radiographs

The routine radiographs of the ankle include a minimum of the anteroposterior (AP) and lateral view. Additional oblique views are occasionally useful for further assessment of subtle injuries, particularly of the talar mortice. Foot injuries require a minimum of an AP and an oblique view. The lateral view is not usually performed as the bones become superimposed, with the exception of the assessment of possible calcaneal injuries. These injuries may also require a dedicated axial calcaneal view. Weight bearing foot or ankle views are rarely of use.

Technical factors

- **Anteroposterior ankle (AP)** film: The AP ankle radiograph is taken with the foot slightly internally rotated so that the fibula does not overlap the lateral joint space.
- **Lateral ankle** film: The lateral radiograph is taken with the X-ray beam centred over the talus. This film should include the calcaneum and base of the fifth metatarsal.
- **Foot** films: The foot radiographs (AP and oblique) are taken with the X-ray beam centred over the midfoot with the foot at least partly dorsiflexed.

Systematic radiological assessment

- The patient's name, date of birth and date on the film should always be checked.
- **Film quality**: As stated, optimal positioning is essential. On the AP ankle view, the fibula should not overlap the talus, and the lateral joint space should be visible. On the lateral ankle view, the whole

of the calcaneum and the base of the fifth metatarsal should be visualised. The oblique foot view should not be over-angulated such that the bones are superimposed, yet it should have a clear obliquity from the AP view.

- **Bone and joint alignment**: On the AP ankle view, the joint space should be uniform and can be followed from the medial side, over the dome of the talus and down the lateral side of the joint (*Figure 12.1*). On the lateral ankle view, the lateral malleolus extends more inferiorly than on the medial side. Also on this view there is a normal line that can be drawn from the posterior aspect of the calcaneum to its highest midpoint. This should intersect a second line drawn from this point to the superior point of the calcaneum anteriorly (*Figure 12.2*). The angle measured between these two lines (termed Bohler's angle) should be 25–40°, and if this is reduced a depressed fracture of the calcaneum is suspected. On the foot views the calcaneum and talus articulate with the cuboid and navicular, respectively. The bases of the first, second and third metatarsals align with the three cuneiform bones. The fourth and fifth metatarsals articulate with the cuboid. Specifically, two normal anatomical lines should always be assessed, one on the AP view, and one on the oblique view; these are termed the Lisfranc lines. On the AP view, the medial margins of both the middle cuneiform and the base of the second metatarsal should align (*Figure 12.3*). On the oblique view the medial margins of both the lateral cuneiform and the base of the third metatarsal should align (*Figure 12.4*).

- **Bony density and margins**: The cortical surfaces of all the visible bones should be systematically examined for irregularities. The internal trabecular pattern should be carefully assessed for subtle radiolucencies or bands of sclerosis, which may be the appearance of an impacted fracture. This is particularly common with fractures of the calcaneum. As with any other bone, the cortices should be smooth and regular, and depressions or steps should be considered as at least suspicious of a fracture.

- **Soft tissues**: Extensive soft tissue swelling around the ankle joint is a common but non-specific sign of trauma, and is often not associated with a bony injury. Soft tissue swelling however often accompanies ligamentous and bony foot injuries.

Common errors in interpretation are listed in *Table 12.1*.

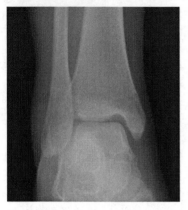

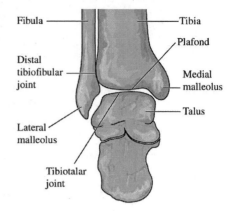

Figure 12.1. A normal AP ankle view and annotated line drawing. The joint space is uniform and can be followed from the medial side, over the dome of the talus and down the lateral side of the joint.

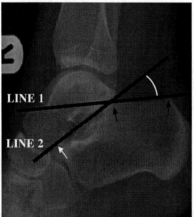

Figure 12.2. Normal lateral ankle view. A normal line (line 1) is drawn from the posterior aspect of the calcaneum to its highest midpoint (black arrows). This intersects a second line (line 2) drawn from the highest midpoint to the superior point of the calcaneum anteriorly (white arrow). A normal Bohler's angle is measured between these two lines (white curved line) and is between 25 and 40 degrees, although if this was reduced a depressed fracture of the calcaneum would be suspected.

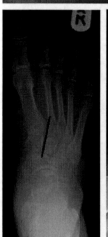
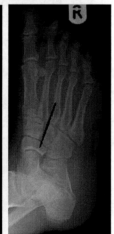

Figure 12.3. (far left) A normal AP view of the foot showing the first Lisfranc line. The medial margins of both the middle cuneiform and the base of the second metatarsal are seen to align (line).

Figure 12.4. (left) A normal oblique view of the foot showing the second Lisfranc line. The medial margins of both the lateral cuneiform and the base of the third metatarsal are seen to align (line).

Table 12.1. Common interpretive errors

- The ankle joint frequently behaves like a ring; a fracture or ligament rupture on one side will often be accompanied by a more subtle break (fracture or rupture) elsewhere
- Medial joint damage (fracture or ligamentous rupture) can be associated with a midshaft or proximal fibula fracture, so this should always be assessed clinically
- A thin sclerotic line may be the only sign of an impacted calcaneal fracture, and so Bohler's angle should always be assessed. However, a normal Bohler's angle does not exclude a calcaneal fracture
- A fracture of the base of the second or third metatarsal should raise clinical suspicion of a midfoot dislocation (Lisfranc injury). Lisfranc's lines should be carefully assessed
- An avulsion fracture of the base of the fifth metatarsal should be distinguished from a normal unfused apophysis
- Beware of black bands of soft tissue margins which may simulate fractures. If a black line crosses a bone and extends beyond the bone it is probably a soft tissue edge or an artefact

Ankle trauma

Ligamentous trauma

Severe ligamentous trauma can produce normal radiographs, although medial ligament rupture often leads to widening of the joint space on the AP view, and is commonly associated with a fracture. The ankle joint and its supporting ligaments frequently behave like a ring; a fracture or ligament rupture on one side will often be accompanied by a more subtle break (fracture or rupture) elsewhere.

Fractures around the ankle

Various mechanisms of injury are responsible for different patterns of ankle fracture too numerous for this chapter, although most are radiographically obvious.

A twisting force will initially produce a spiral fracture of the distal fibula (*Figure 12.5*), but if more severe this will be accompanied by rupture of the medial ligament or a medial malleolus avulsion (*Figure 12.6*), and if extreme the posterior malleolus may also be avulsed. Sometimes this fracture will pass through the distal tibiofibular joint, which may become widened. Any distal fibula fracture at this level should be considered as potentially involving this joint even if there is no joint space widening, as it may subsequently displace during the healing period. These injuries therefore require careful conservative management and follow up radiographs.

An inversion force will initially result in a lateral ligament rupture, then a lateral malleolus avulsion and finally a compression fracture of the medial malleolus. Accessory ossicles are commonly sited near the malleoli, and can sometimes be difficult to distinguish radiographically, although they are typically well defined with a sclerotic margin.

Occasionally medial joint damage (fracture or ligamentous rupture) is associated with a midshaft or proximal fibula fracture, so this should always be assessed clinically and if there is doubt, a full lower leg radiograph can be performed (Maissoneuve fracture). In a patient with an apparent isolated medial or posterior malleolar injury and a radiographically normal lateral malleolus, this injury should be strongly considered.

In children, as with other joints, epiphyseal plate fractures are common.

More severe injuries include complete ankle dislocation.

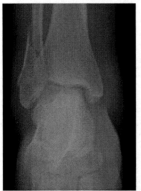

Figure 12.5. An AP view of the ankle showing a spiral fracture of the distal fibula. Soft tissue swelling is present on the medial side of the joint, although no fracture is seen and the medial joint space is not widened to suggest a ligamentous injury. However these injuries should be treated with suspicion as an occult medial ligament injury is common and the mortice may later displace.

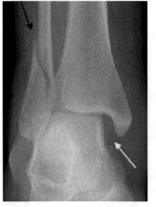

Figure 12.6. AP view of the ankle showing a spiral fracture of the distal fibula (black arrow) accompanied by rupture of the medial ligament as shown by widening of the medial joint space (white arrow). This injury is unstable and surgical correction is usually required.

Talus fractures

Like the scaphoid bone in the wrist, a fracture of the talus may result in avascular necrosis since the body receives its blood supply from the distal aspect (head). Therefore a fracture of the waist may result in avascular necrosis of the body. Osteochondral fractures of the talar dome can be identified by either a small defect in the upper cortex of the talus, or a bone fragment within the ankle joint (*Figure 12.7*).

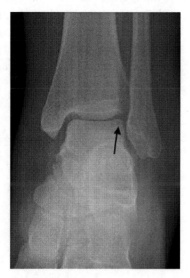

Figure 12.7. An AP view of the ankle showing an osteochondral fracture of the talar dome which is identified as a small defect in the upper cortex of the talus (arrow).

Foot trauma

Calcaneal fractures

While calcaneal fractures may occur from a simple twisting injury, a fall from a height is the commonest mechanism of injury, and it is often associated with spinal fractures. In the latter situation the fractures are often obvious on a lateral foot view, but a dedicated axial view may be required (*Figures 12.8, 12.9*). Some are less obvious and Bohler's angle should then be assessed (*Figure 12.2*); an angle of less than 25 degrees indicates a depressed fracture which may be impacted and only visible as a thin sclerotic line.

Midfoot injuries

With the exception of avulsion fractures of the navicular (*Figure 12.10*), tarsal fractures are uncommon, frequently resulting from severe trauma. They are often associated with severe ligamentous damage, and are difficult to assess clinically and on plain radiographs. Familiarity with the normal tarsal and metatarsal alignment is important, although computed tomography is frequently required. Fractures of the bases of the medial four metatarsals should raise suspicion for a midfoot dislocation, particularly if the normal anatomical Lisfranc lines are disrupted. A homolateral type Lisfranc injury involves a fracture of the base of the second metatarsal with dislocation of the second to fifth metatarsals laterally, resulting in malalignment of the normal metatarsal and cuneiform bones (*Figure 12.11*). This can also occur with fractures at the base of the third metatarsal with similar associated metatarsal dislocations. Occasionally the first metatarsal may dislocate medially while the second to fifth metatarsals move laterally; this is termed a divergent type Lisfranc fracture dislocation, and is more common in patients with diabetic neuropathy. This type may also be associated with fracture/dislocation of the medial cuneiform and navicular.

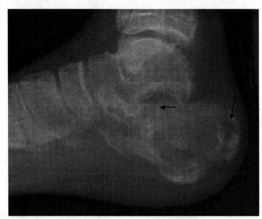

Figure 12.8. A lateral view of the foot showing a calcaneal fracture (arrows). The calcaneum is clearly flattened and Bohler's angle is much less than 25 degrees (see Figure 12.2).

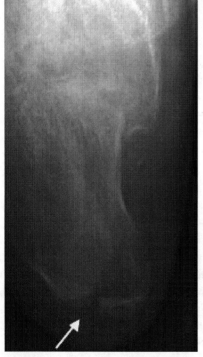

Figure 12.9. (left) An axial view of the calcaneum showing a calcaneal fracture (arrow). This dedicated view is essential if the fracture is not clear on the lateral view. Calcaneal fractures may sometimes be subtle, with only a thin sclerotic line visible.

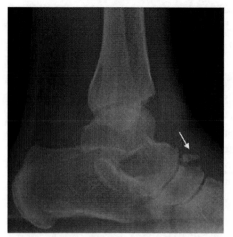

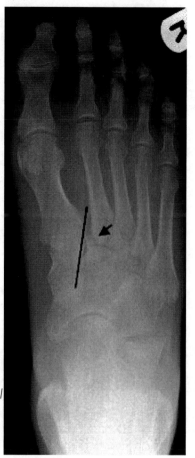

Figure 12.10. (above)A lateral view of the foot showing an avulsion fracture of the navicular (arrow). Isolated tarsal fractures such as this are uncommon.

Figure 12.11. (right) An AP view of the foot showing a fracture of the base of the second metatarsal (arrow) and malalignment of the normal anatomical first Lisfranc line (line), indicating an associated ligamentous rupture. This injury may appear slight, but a homolateral type Lisfranc fracture dislocation of the midfoot is a severe injury and computed tomography may be required for full assessment.

Forefoot injuries

An avulsion fracture of the base of the fifth metatarsal usually results from an ankle inversion injury (*Figure 12.12*). This should be distinguished from a normal unfused apophysis (*Figure 12.13*). This fracture is often visualised on the standard ankle views, although clinical examination will allow more appropriate foot views to be taken.

Fractures of the shafts of the metatarsals are commonly 'stress' fractures and are due to repetitive minor trauma (classically marching in young soldiers; this is also termed a march fracture). A thick periosteal reaction surrounding the second metatarsal is a common appearance, although these radiographic appearances may take weeks to develop (*Figure 12.14*). An MRI or an isotope bone scan will demonstrate a stress fracture before it becomes radiographically apparent.

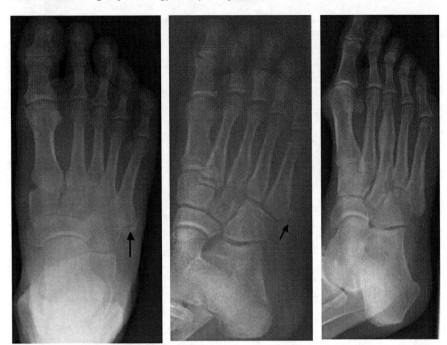

Figure 12.12. (left) An AP view of the foot showing a fracture of the base of the fifth metatarsal (arrow). This most commonly results from an inversion injury, and is usually an avulsion fracture at the insertion of the peroneus brevis tendon.
Figure 12.13. (centre) An oblique view of the foot showing a normal unfused apophysis at the base of the fifth metatarsal (arrow). This is a common finding especially in young patients and should be distinguished from a fracture. The apophysis lies parallel to the long axis of the metatarsal, as opposed to a fracture, which is usually transverse (see Figure 12.12).
Figure 12.14. (right) An oblique view of the foot showing a thick periosteal reaction surrounding the third metatarsal, consistent with a stress fracture due to repetitive minor trauma. Although this is a common appearance, these radiographic appearances may take weeks to develop.

Further imaging

Increasingly, computed tomography is being utilised in the further assessment of more complex injuries to the foot and ankle. This is becoming particularly more common in the context of preoperative surgical planning where surgeons can be provided with three dimensional images of the injury prior to surgery (*Figure 12.15*).

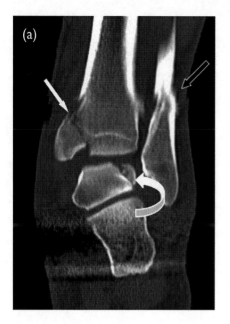 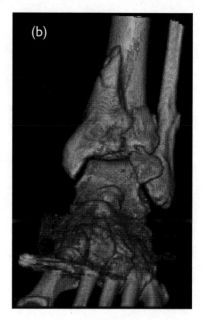

Figure 12.15. (a) A coronal reconstructed computed tomography image showing a left ankle fracture. There is a fracture through the distal tibia (white arrow), distal fibula (black arrow) and lateral talar dome (curved arrow). (b) The computed tomography image in (a) has been combined with multiple other images through this joint and been reconstructed using a computer workstation to produce this three-dimensional image called a surface shaded display. This shows a comminuted fracture of the distal tibia and a simple fracture through the distal fibula. This type of image is often extremely useful to orthopaedic surgeons prior to planning reconstructive surgery.

Key points

- Always check the patient's name and age and date of the film
- Assess film quality
- Assess the bony cortices of the talar dome, calcaneum and the base of the fifth metatarsal for subtle fractures on the ankle radiograph
- Assess the alignment of the medial margins of the second and third metatarsals with the medial margins of the middle and lateral cuneiforms, respectively
- An MR or an isotope bone scan will demonstrate a stress fracture before it becomes radiographically apparent

CHAPTER 13

Foreign bodies

Introduction

Foreign bodies may be swallowed, inhaled, inserted or introduced accidently or non-accidently. Radiography should always be performed after removal to determine if any pieces remain.

Glass

All glass is radio-opaque. A skin marker should be applied over the laceration prior to X-ray as small glass splinters may be easily missed. A soft tissue technique will help render a glass fragment more conspicuous. Two views are necessary as bones may mask glass fragments (*Figure 13.1*).

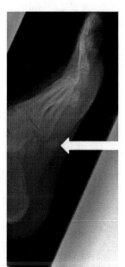

Wood and plastic

Wood and plastic are usually radiolucent and therefore radiography is not useful. Ultrasound (*Figure 13.2*) is the modality of choice in the detection and removal.

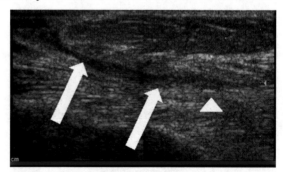

Figure 13.1. Lateral view of the foot showing a fragment of glass (arrow) which could not be visualised on the AP view (not shown).

Figure 13.2. Ultrasound of a subcutaneous 3mm wooden splinter (between callipers indicated by an arrowhead) with a tract leading to it from the skin surface (arrows). It was successfully removed using ultrasound guidance. Courtesy of Dr Pilcher, Consultant Radiologist, St George's Hospital, London

Fish and chicken bones

Swallowed bones usually lodge in the laryngopharynx or upper oesophagus. Generally only a lateral view of the neck is necessary for detection using a soft tissue exposure (*Figure 13.3*). The anatomy of this area can be difficult to interpret. The laryngeal cartilages may calcify with a wide spectrum of normal appearances. The hyoid bone and stylohyoid ligament, which may partially or completely ossify/calcify, respectively, should be identified. The epiglottis may be visualised as a soft tissue swelling in cases of acute epiglottitis. The pre-vertebral soft tissues measure up to 7mm from C1 to C4 and below C4 the width of a vertebral body (up to 22mm in adults or 14mm in children).

All chicken bones are radio-opaque but may be difficult to see. If in doubt show the film to an experienced clinician or radiologist.

Fish bones vary in their calcium content and therefore in their radio-opacity. Cod and haddock bones are easily seen, whereas salmon, herring, trout and kipper bones are radiolucent.

Indirect signs of the presence of a foreign body that should be sought are gas formation (abscess), prevertebral soft tissue swelling, surgical emphysema or loss of the normal cervical lordosis due to muscular spasm.

In the presence of stridor the foreign body should be removed urgently. If the radiograph is normal and the patient is clinically well he or she may be discharged home and advised to return if symptoms persist or get worse. The patient should be referred to an ear, nose and throat surgeon if he or she is clinically unwell, if a foreign body is seen on the radiograph or if the patient re-attends casualty.

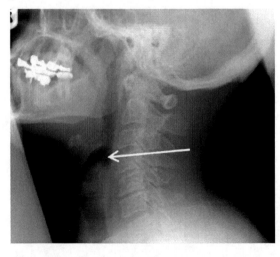

Figure 13.3. Lateral view of the neck using a soft tissue exposure showing a fishbone (arrow).

Swallowed objects

Coins and other small objects will usually be passed spontaneously if they get past the oesophagus. In children a single well-penetrated chest X-ray (including the neck) should be sufficient. In adults a chest X-ray and possibly a lateral view are necessary to ascertain the position of the coin (*Figure 13.4*). Abdominal films are unnecessary in either children or adults. The coins presently in circulation in the UK are inert.

Sharp or potentially dangerous objects need to be located. These include dentures, pins/needles, razors and batteries. These pose a risk of bowel obstruction, perforation and ensuing complications such as peritonitis and mediastinitis. An abdominal X-ray should be initially performed (*Figure 13.5, 13.6*). If this is normal a chest X-ray and lateral chest X-ray should be obtained. If these are normal, computed tomography (*Figure 13.7*) or endoscopy should be considered.

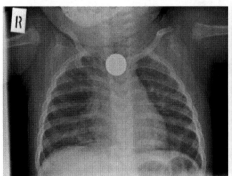
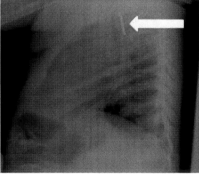
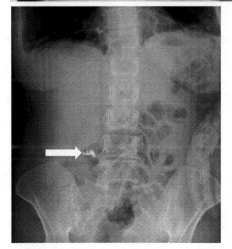

Figure 13.4. (above) Frontal and lateral chest radiograph showing a coin (arrow) stuck in the upper oesophagus. Note the air lucency of the trachea anterior to the coin on the lateral view confirming its position in the oesophagus.

Figure 13.5. (left) Abdominal film showing a dental bridge (arrow) which had been accidently swallowed during intubation. It was passed rectally without incident.

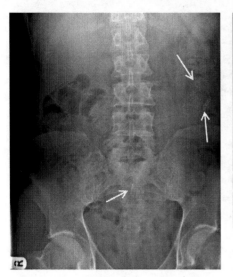

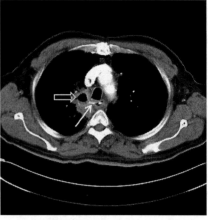

Figure 13.7. Axial CT chest showing a chicken bone (arrow) which had perforated the oesophagus resulting in mediastinitis and abscess formation (unfilled arrow).

Figure 13.6. Abdominal film showing multiple razor blades (arrows) which had been intentionally swallowed by a psychiatric patient. They were passed with minimal rectal bleeding.

Rectal objects

According to size and nature, surgical referral is suggested to ascertain whether the object may be removed manually or under anaesthetic (*Figure 13.8*).

Orbital foreign bodies

The majority of foreign bodies can be detected using a slit lamp. For metal and glass fragments radiography may be useful. Two views are obtained (upward and downward gaze). If the foreign body moves it is situated within the globe. Additional imaging should only be performed after ophthalmology consultation. Ultrasound or CT may be useful to localise identified foreign bodies or detect radiolucent objects.

Miscellaneous

Plain film radiography may be useful to locate superficial foreign bodies following head injuries (*Figure 13.9*), road traffic accidents, assaults and gunshot wounds (*Figure 13.10*).

In penetrating or blunt trauma to the chest CT is the modality of choice in a haemodynamically stable patient. In abdominal trauma ultrasound or CT is indicated in haemodynamically stable patients while unstable patients require urgent surgery.

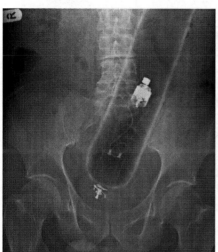

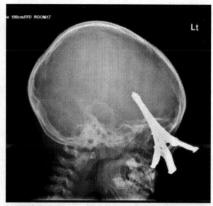

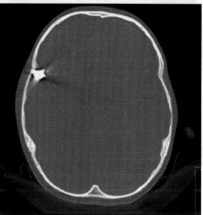

Figure 13.8. Large rectal foreign body which had been inserted during a stag weekend. It required surgical removal.

Figure 13.9. (above right, right) Lateral skull and CT brain (on bone windows) of a 3-year-old boy who fell on a metal model of the Eiffel Tower which penetrated his skull. Fortunately it was removed without ill effect. Courtesy of Dr Pilcher, Consultant Radiologist, St George's Hospital, London

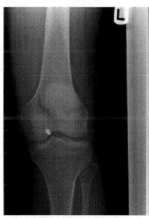

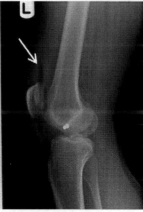

Figure 13.10. Knee radiographs showing an intra-articular bullet. Note the air fluid level (arrow) due to a haemarthrosis.

Key points

- Glass and metal are radio-opaque and therefore are best detected by plain film radiography
- Wood and plastic are best detected by ultrasound
- Ultrasound is the best modality to guide removal of superficial foreign bodies
- A lateral soft tissue neck radiograph is best to detect fish and chicken bones. Patients should be referred to an ENT surgeon if they are unwell, a foreign body is seen or if they represent to casualty
- Swallowed coins and small blunt objects usually do not cause problems once they pass the oesophagus. A chest X-ray is indicated to ascertain whether they are lodged in the oesophagus. Abdominal radiography is unnecessary
- Ingested sharp objects should be localised with abdomianl X-ray and/ or chest X-ray. CT may be necessary in complex cases
- For orbital foreign bodies slit lamp examination will detect the majority of foreign bodies. After ophthalmological consultation plain films may be useful in detection of glass or metal fragments. Ultrasound or CT is useful for wood or plastic
- Radiography must always be performed after foreign body removal to determine whether any piece remains

CHAPTER 14

Paediatric trauma

With contributions from Dr Jackie Hughes (Consultant Radiologist, Addenbrooke's Hospital, Cambridge) and P Bhakoo (Superintendent Radiographer, Department of Imaging, West Middlesex Hospital, London, UK)

Introduction

Fractures in children differ from those in adults in a number of ways (Thornton and Gyll, 1999; Carty, 2002; Strouse, 2008). The immature skeleton is more elastic resulting in incomplete fractures (torus and greenstick) as well as fractures without cortical disruption. In addition the periosteum is more elastic and thicker than in adults. Also children's bones heal quicker and remodel more readily. However, there are areas of structural weakness, which adults do not possess, in the epiphyseal growth plates and zones of cartilage hypertrophy. Therefore fractures at these sites are common.

This chapter will describe the common types and sites of paediatric bone injuries as well as a brief review of non-accidental injury.

Types of paediatric injuries

Greenstick fracture

This fracture is characterised by a break in one cortex and bending of the other (*Figure 14.1*) and usually results from an angulation force.

Torus fracture

This a variant of the greenstick fracture where buckling of the cortices is seen (*Figure 14.2*). This type of injury results from a longitudinal compression force. The commonest sites for this injury are the distal radius and ulna. Angulation is usually not seen with this injury.

Plastic bowing fracture

In this type of injury bending of the bones is seen without cortical break (*Figure 14.1*). Subtle fractures may be missed initially and only become apparent when new periosteal bone forms along the shaft.

Growth plate injuries: Salter-Harris Classification

The epiphysis, epiphyseal plate and metaphysis is involved in up to 15% of fractures of the long bones in children. The epiphyseal plate is weaker than the adjacent ligaments and tendons and so is commonly involved in injuries. The complication of premature epiphyseal fusion may lead to angulation deformities (if part of the growth plate is involved) or limb shortening.

The Salter-Harris classification of epiphyseal injuries should be known and applied (*Table 14.1, Figure 14.3*). The type II fracture is the most common type. As a rule of thumb the lower the Salter-Harris number the better the prognosis (*Figures 14.4, 14.5, 14.6, 14.7*).

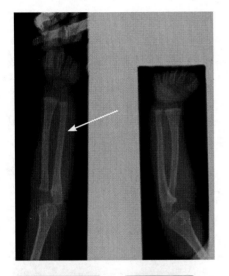

Figure 14.1. AP and lateral radiographs of the forearm showing a greenstick fracture of the ulna (arrow) and plastic bowing of the radius.

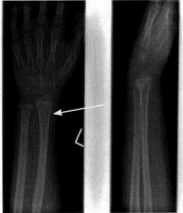

Figure 14.2. Torus fracture (arrow) of the distal radius seen as buckling of the cortext.

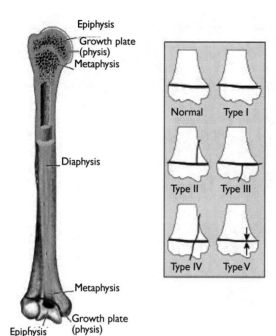

Figure 14.3. Salter-Harris Classification of epiphyseal plate injuries.

Table 14.1. Salter-Harris Classification

Type I: Separation of the epiphysis with the fracture confined to the growth plate (6%). Examples include apophyseal avulsion and slipped capital femoral epiphysis. This has a good prognosis regardless of site

Type II: Fracture through the growth plate extending through the metaphysis (75%). This type of fracture is usually seen at the distal radius. It has a good prognosis but may result in minimal shortening

Type III: Fracture through the growth plate extending through the epiphysis (8%) and into the joint space. The prognosis is fair

Type IV: Fracture extending from the articular surface of the epiphysis (i.e. involving the joint space) through the growth plate and metaphysis (10%). There is an increased likelihood of deformity and angulation

Type V: Compression of the growth plate (1%). The prognosis is poor with growth impairment very common

The prognosis is worse in the lower limb, independent of Salter-Harris type

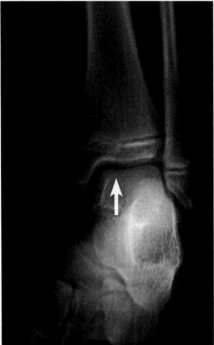

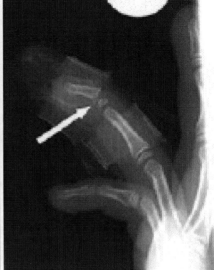

Figure 14.5. Salter-Harris types I and II fractures of the distal phalanx of the index finger (arrow). The type I injury is manifest as slip of the epiphysis.

Figure 14.4. Salter-Harris type III fracture (arrow) of the distal tibial epiphysis. Reproduced with permission from Harvey et al. (2005) Self-Assessment Cases in Surgical Imaging. Oxford University Press.

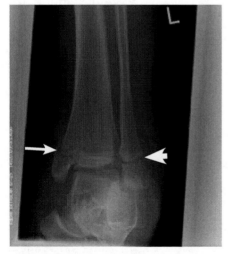

Figure 14.6. Salter-Harris types II and IV fractures of the ankle. The type IV injury is seen of the medial malleolus (thick arrow) and the type II injury of the lateral malleolus (chevron).

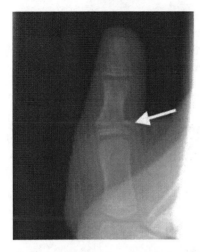

Figure 14.7. Salter-Harris type II fracture of the base of the proximal phalanx of the thumb (arrow).

Common paediatric injuries

During birth (most frequently in breech deliveries) fractures and dislocations can occur, particularly in the skull and clavicles. During the first two years fractures are rare and may raise the possibility of non-accidental injury. After the age of 2 fractures of the radius, phalanges and metacarpals are common. Supracondylar and toddler's fractures are also common in the 2–5 year age group.

Specific paediatric trauma will now be discussed.

Supracondylar fractures

Supracondylar fractures are the commonest elbow fracture in children and are usually caused by a fall on an outstretched hand. Usually a transverse fracture passes just proximal to the capitellum and trochlea, with the distal fragment often posteriorly displaced. On a lateral view a line traced along the anterior cortex of the humerus should bisect the capitellum such that one third lies anterior to this line. In a supracondylar fracture posterior displacement of the distal fracture fragment results in the line lying anterior to the capitellum (*Figure 14.8*). Undisplaced fractures are often missed, but a positive posterior fad pad sign is almost always present.

Epicondylar elbow injuries

Epicondyle injuries are also common, and can be extensive, involving also the capitellum, trochlea and distal humeral metaphysis. Internal (medial) epicondylar epiphyseal avulsions occur in relation to elbow dislocations

(*Figure 14.9*). The avulsed epiphysis is usually displaced inferiorly, but it may lie intra-articularly. In this situation it may be misinterpreted as being one of the other ossification centres. Remembering the normal sequence of ossification will assist diagnosis and is denoted by the acronym CRITOL (Capitellum: 1 year; Radial head: 3 years; Internal (medial) epicondyle: 5 years; Trochlea: 9–11 years; Olecranon: 9–11 years; and Lateral (external)

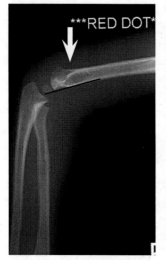

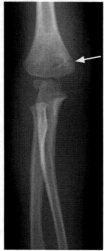

Figure 14.8. (left) AP and lateral radiographs of the elbow showing a supracondylar fracture (arrow). Note that a line drawn along the anterior humeral surface would pass anterior to the capitellum. The presence of a posterior fat pad (thick arrow) is indicative of a joint effusion.

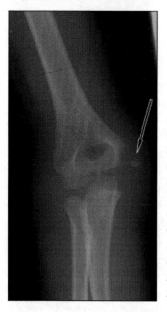

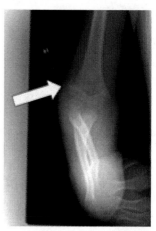

Figure 14.9. (left) AP elbow radiograph showing an internal epicondylar epiphyseal avulsion. The avulsed epiphysis is displaced inferiorly (black arrow), and occurred due to sudden valgus stress.

Figure 14.10. (above) AP elbow radiograph showing a lateral epicondylar fracture (arrow) as part of a supracondylar fracture.

epicondyle: 9–11 years). If the trochlear epiphysis is present, the internal epicondyle epiphysis must also be present on the radiograph and may be avulsed. A positive fat pad sign may help, and in difficult cases a radiograph of the uninjured side may be of use. Fracture of the lateral epicondyle is the second most common fracture of the elbow in children (*Figure 14.10*).

Pulled elbow (Nursemaid's elbow)

Pulled elbow occurs in children between 1 and 4 years of age, and occurs when there is a sudden pull on the pronated extended arm, such as when the child is suddenly lifted by the hand. It occurs due to momentary distraction of the radiocapitellar joint, producing subluxation of the radial head through the angular ligament. Reduction is achieved by supinating the forearm. Radiographs are usually normal.

Avulsion fractures

Fractures of the apophyses (secondary ossification centres) at the tendinous insertions are usually seen in young athletes. Typically there is irregularity at the site of injury with avulsed pieces of bone of variable size. Common avulsion sites and the tendon insertions are the anterior superior iliac spine (sartorius) (*Figure 14.11*), anterior inferior iliac spine (rectus femoris), greater trochanter (gluteal muscles), lesser trochanter (psoas), ischial tuberosity (hamstrings) and pubic tubercle (adductors).

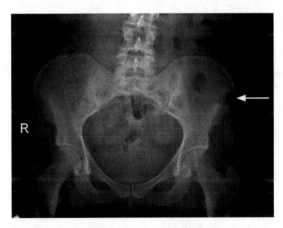

Figure 14.11. Old avulsion of the left anterior superior iliac spine in a mature skeleton (arrow).

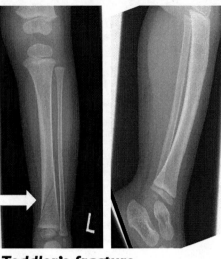

Figure 14.12. AP and lateral radiographs of the leg showing a Toddler's fracture (arrow) which is best seen on the AP view.

Toddler's fracture

This is caused by falling with one leg stationary (e.g. between the bars of a cot) and results in a spiral fracture of the tibia (*Figure 14.12*).

Tibial stress fractures

The proximal tibial shaft is the most common site of stress fractures in children. They are seen at 10 days as a dense sclerotic band across all or part of the shaft followed by variable periostitis.The sclerotic change may be replaced by a radiolucent band. Magnetic resonance imaging (MRI) and nuclear scanning will detect the abnormality as early as 3 days post-onset of symptoms.

Slipped femoral capital epiphysis

Slipped femoral capital epiphysis (SCFE) is the commonest adolescent hip disorder with boys affected two to three times more than girls. SCFE is a Salter-Harris type I fracture. Classically the condition occurs in obese boys at ages 10–17. The condition is bilateral in 20–40% and therefore all patients should be closely followed up because about 25% develop a slip of the contralateral hip within 18 months of the first slip. The slip is usually posteromedial with decreased epiphyseal height, widening and irregularity of the growth plate on the anteroposterior (AP) film. A line (Klein's line) drawn along the lateral femoral neck should intersect the capital epiphysis so that one-sixth of it lies lateral to the line. In 10% of cases no abnormality is present on the AP film but the frog-leg view is usually diagnostic (*Figure 14.13*).

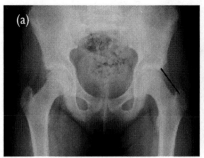 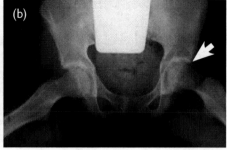

Figure 14.13. Left slipped capital femoral epiphysis (SCFE). There is posterior slip of the left capital femoral epiphysis. A straight line drawn along the lateral margin of the femoral neck should normally transect the superior aspect of the femoral epiphysis. On the AP view (a) the left femoral epiphysis is not transected by this line. The frog-leg view (b) clearly shows the slip of the left capital femoral epiphysis. Reproduced with permission from Harvey et al. (2005) Self-Assessment Cases in Surgical Imaging. Oxford University Press.

Hip pain

Hip pain is the commonest cause of paediatric orthopaedic admissions in the UK. The majority of these children are diagnosed as having a transient synovitis (irritable hip) which is a self-limiting condition, seen throughout childhood, associated with an effusion and thought to be viral in aetiology. Other more serious conditions need to be excluded. These include septic arthritis, inflammatory arthritis, Perthes' disease (idiopathic avascular necrosis which is commoner in boys and rare over the age of 7 years) and a slipped femoral capital epiphysis. Remember that hip pain may be referred to the knee in children so X-ray the hip if necessary as well as the knee in children presenting with knee pain.

In the investigation of hip pain some centres initially perform a plain radiograph of the pelvis as well as frog-leg view. If this is normal an ultrasound is performed with aspiration of a joint effusion for microbiological analysis. All children should be reviewed one week later in the orthopaedic or paediatric clinic where further investigations such as MRI may be performed to exclude conditions such as septic arthritis, Perthes' disease or stress fractures. In other departments an ultrasound is performed first followed by plain radiography if the ultrasound is normal.

Non-accidental injury

Non-accidental injury (NAI) should be considered in all children presenting to a casualty department with an injury. Of these cases 80% occur before the age of 2 years. Fractures occur in approximately 50% and are typically multiple, in varying stages of healing (some with periosteal reaction and others with mature callus) and are not explained by a plausible history. Subperiosteal new bone formation may be caused by subperiosteal bleeding due to shaking or squeezing and will become radiographically apparent weeks after the injury (*Figure 14.14*). Shaft fractures are more common than metaphyseal fractures but the latter are virtually pathognomic. The corner fracture (or bucket handle) of a metaphysis (*Figure 14.15*) is due to tractional or torsional stresses on the limbs and occurs in the long bones. Rib fractures, especially posterior ones, in a child under 2 years are virtually pathognomic of NAI (*Figures 14.14, 14.16*). They result from violent shaking or squeezing episodes and are a recognised association with brain injury and therefore are an indication for computed tomography (CT) of the brain. Other fractures, which have a high specificity for abuse, include fractures of the scapula, small bones of the hands and feet, pelvis, sternum, vertebral compression and transverse processes. Skull fractures, especially depressed occipital fractures, are highly suggestive. If NAI is suspected senior paediatric advice should be sought.

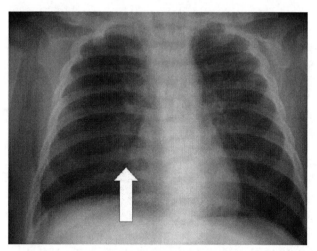

Figure 14.14. This 18-month-old child was brought to casualty with a cough. The bilateral clavicular and posterior right 8th rib fractures (arrow) were noted. Further investigation confirmed non-accidental injury. Courtesy of Dr N Davies, Consultant Radiologist, Worthing Hospital, West Sussex, UK.

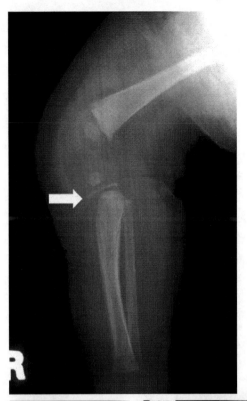

Figure 14.15. Bucket handle
fracture (arrow) of the proximal
tibial metaphysis is due to
tractional or torsional stresses
on the limbs and are virtually
pathognomic of non-accidental
injury.

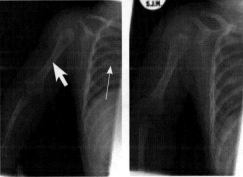

Figure 14.16. A proven case of non-accidental
injury with a right posterior 6th rib fracture
(thin arrow) and a fracture of the mid shaft
of the humerus with associated periosteal
reaction (thick arrow). Courtesy of Dr A Lim,
Consultant Radiologist, Charing Cross Hospital,
London, UK.

Key points

- The immature skeleton is more elastic than the adult skeleton resulting in incomplete fractures such as torus, greenstick and plastic bowing injuries
- Know the Salter-Harris classification of epiphyseal injuries. The type of injury is of prognostic value
- Supracondylar fractures are the commonest elbow fracture in children. They are one of the most important paediatric arm injuries due to associated brachial artery and median or ulnar nerve injury
- In suspected slipped femoral capital epiphysis (SCFE) a frog-leg view should always be performed
- 80% of non-accidental injury (NAI) occurs before the age of 2 years. Characteristic bone injuries of NAI include multiple injuries, in varying stages of healing and not explained by a plausible history, posterior rib fractures, metaphyseal corner and depressed occipital fractures

References

Carty H (2002) *Emergency Paediatric Radiology.* Berlin, Springer

Strouse P (2008) Paediatric trauma. In: Thomas L Slovis (ed.) *Musculoskeletal System. Section VI: Caffey's Pediatric Diagnostic Imaging.* 11th edn. St Louis, Mosby

Thornton A, Gyll C (1999) *Children's Fractures. A Radiological Guide to Safe Practice.* Philadelphia, W B Saunders

Index